To Elizabeth
    From Mommy and Daddy
Christmas 1999

Christian Dior

Christian Dior

Richard Martin and Harold Koda

Photographs by Karin L. Willis

The Metropolitan Museum of Art, New York
Distributed by Harry N. Abrams, Inc., New York

This volume has been published in conjunction with the exhibition "Christian Dior," held at The Metropolitan Museum of Art from December 12, 1996, through March 23, 1997.

The exhibition and the accompanying publication are made possible by **Christian Dior** and L V M H / MOËT HENNESSY LOUIS VUITTON.

Published by The Metropolitan Museum of Art, New York
Copyright © 1996 by The Metropolitan Museum of Art, New York

John P. O'Neill, Editor in Chief
Barbara Cavaliere, Editor
Design by Matsumoto Incorporated, New York
Matthew Pimm, Production Manager
Robert Weisberg, Computer Specialist

Library of Congress Cataloging-in-Publication Data

Christian Dior / Richard Martin and Harold Koda.
          p.   cm.
       "Published in conjunction with the exhibition 'Christian Dior,' held at The Metropolitan Museum of Art from December 12, 1996, through March 23, 1997."
       Includes bibliographical references.
       ISBN 0-87099-822-6 (cloth). —
       ISBN 0-87099-823-4 (pbk.). —
       ISBN 0-8109-6506-2 (Abrams)
       1. Dior, Christian—Exhibitions.
2. Costume design—France—History—20th century—Exhibitions. 3. Fashion—France—History—20th century—Exhibitions. I. Koda, Harold. II. Metropolitan Museum of Art (New York, N.Y.). III. Title.
746.9'2'092—dc21   96-45943
                                         CIP

The photography in this volume is by Karin L. Willis, The Photograph Studio, The Metropolitan Museum of Art.

Printed by Meridian Printing, East Greenwich, Rhode Island

Cover. Dinner dress, fall-winter 1949. See also page 65.

Frontispiece. "May" evening dress, detail, 1953. See also pages 120 and 121.

Note: All the costumes illustrated in this publication are in the collection of The Costume Institute, The Metropolitan Museum of Art.

Contents

Sponsor's Statement

It is with great pleasure that Christian Dior supports The Metropolitan Museum of Art on the occasion of The Costume Institute's exhibition "Christian Dior," a tribute to the timeless fashion masterpieces from the decade when Monsieur Dior designed for the House.

Christian Dior's creation of the "New Look" in 1947 revolutionized fashion, reestablished Paris as the focal point of the fashion world, and secured Dior as a name symbolic of elegance, impeccable quality, and continuous modernity. As we commemorate the fiftieth anniversary of the House of Dior, we are proud to celebrate the legacy of that success and bring this creative spirit into a new century.

Bernard Arnault

Foreword

At the waning of this century, we take the occasion of the fiftieth anniversary of Christian Dior's "New Look" to review the magnificent work he created in a little more than one decade at the century's heart. Few occasions in fashion history are as precise, and few are as worthy of consideration and celebration.

It is difficult to analyze Dior today: the intervening four decades have irrevocably distanced us from his circumstances and his world. The Museum has consciously chosen to present neither a biography nor a retrospective. Without intruding ourselves too much into this history, we seek to see Dior as a genial creator. His idealized conceptualization of woman must be understood as a campaign of hope and optimism in which, in fact, most women of his time participated willingly. This exhibition also underscores the ever young character of the work: the Dior *jeune fille* is always as fresh as his beloved flowers.

The exhibition and book have arisen from the unrivaled collection of Dior's work in The Costume Institute. Every garment in the book comes from the Museum. They were assembled chiefly from the collections of stylish and beneficent New Yorkers and generous donations from Christian Dior himself. Our Diors represent but one great strength of The Costume Institute. No other clothing archive in the world equals ours in the depth and breadth of its holdings.

Pride of possession and pride in the New Yorkers and other benefactors who made our collection possible are only part of the reason for this project. We also accept a responsibility for critical evaluation, interpretation, and exhibition. We have chosen an expository, artifact-based consideration of Dior that directs us to the objects. The photographic details and precise accounts of those garments in the pages of this book shed light on the absolute mastery of a craft put at the service of a brilliantly creative imagination. For sponsorship of the exhibition and catalogue, we are most grateful for the generous support of Christian Dior and LVMH/Moët Hennessy Louis Vuitton.

For some viewers in 1996-97, Christian Dior's work is a cherished memory. Others, many younger, may be seeing these masterpieces for the first time. For both, this analytical study from our collection promises revelations and delivers what Dior always produced, extraordinary beauty.

Philippe de Montebello
Director
The Metropolitan Museum of Art

Introduction

"...fashion comes from a dream..."
Christian Dior

Implying the absolute dignity befitting its creator and referring to the flower, also appropriate to its creator's interests, Christian Dior's first collection was titled "Corolle," denoting its flowerlike silhouettes. History, seizing on the enthusiastic locution coined by *Harper's Bazaar* editor Carmel Snow, eagerly called it "The New Look." Never before and never since has fashion so definitively and so aptly described a time.

Precise in its historical function, Dior's New Look has become the rubric by which we identify not only that first collection but also the full span of Dior's work from 1947 through 1957. It is difficult to distinguish Dior's earlier couture work for Lucien Lelong from that of Pierre Balmain and other designers active in that atelier. Hence, we have only a decade of work attributed with certainty to Dior. To view it as generic of The New Look is both illuminating and misleading. After all, the designer exerted great effort to distinguish each collection by name and by nuance, or even by notable differentiation. Yet there are characteristics that we see that are indicative of the entire decade's work. It is very like describing Picasso's adventure through Analytical Cubism, which, though achieved with shifts and variations, ultimately is always describing the one and only Picasso. There is a constancy in Dior's work, despite the marketable change within its continuity. There is a nucleus in his creation around which all change revolves or, at most, evolves. The designer's insistence on a separate name for each collection is not a falsehood, nor is it merely a service to marketing. But finally, these collections are the benchmarks of a single journey, divisible parts of a single philosophical whole.

This eleven-year corpus, then, defines a life's work. Many have described and recounted that life, a relatively privileged and aesthetic one, and even Dior himself gave considerable credit to his life circumstances as the conditions for his art.

But Dior's work, perceived paramountly through the garments themselves, encompasses more than its creator. It speaks so eloquently and powerfully on its fiftieth anniversary not because of the life of its maker but because of its essential place in the life and history of the twentieth century. Dior was an optimist of sorts. His writings breathe with a hopeful aestheticism; he believed in beauty and offered beauty, however uncertainly defined, as a force in the world. His collections convey a will to believe, a sure confidence in the unsure world of the 1940s and 1950s. No garments have ever expressed hope as unquestionably as Dior's.

In the wake of war and holocaust, Dior offered not merely a new look but also a new faith. His first collection and those of the succeeding decade purveyed fashion in denotation of the feminine and the opulent. His surety in each overall silhouette and in collection silhouettes was the postwar antidote to the loss of fashion incurred during the war. Moreover, Dior's assertion of a strong silhouette came at a time and place of utmost fragility. Paris reclaimed its stature as an international capital of fashion after World War II largely through the triumphant success of Dior, even as the School of Paris had decamped and French letters seemed in hibernation. In 1947, the unequivocal certainty that Dior posed came as a relief to those who saw style in disarray, as uniforms of military and civilian service for women were only gradually being replaced by the clothing of dreams. The fashion fantasy Dior propagated was an old one, but one that was especially welcome in a war-weary world. Art historian Rémy Saisselin argued in 1959, on Dior's positing, that "a dress by Dior, like a poem by Valéry, is a feast of the intellect." Dior promoted a conception of fashion as a consummate and ultimate art, equivalent to the other products of French civilization before and after World War II.

This book presents a suite of garments by Dior from 1947 through 1957. Inevitably, we acknowledge the chiefly American collectors and wearers who, in most cases, gave them to The Metropolitan Museum of Art. For some, these designs were the attire of daily life or of party occasions, not a self-conscious art. For others, such as Saisselin, they constitute poetry. For still others, these dresses were the signs that the life-menacing hemorrhages of war and evil had been stanched.

We count the years, collections, and garments of Dior knowing that they comprise a mighty force of convictions about beauty and civilization. To say of any or all in our inventory that they endow life with beauty, poetry, or hope is a prodigious claim for pieces of cloth. Yet, in Dior's case, they do.

1947

"Chérie" dinner dress, detail, spring-summer 1947. Sapphire-blue changeant silk taffeta. Gift of Christian Dior, 1948 (CI 48.13 a,b). See also page 15.

This virtuoso achievement in dressmaking was reached by the compression of vast volume into an adjoining sculptural reduction. "Chérie" contains over thirteen-and-one-half yards of fabric that are pleated into the wasp waist. The accomplishment of grand to mince is possible only because of the couture's expert manipulation of cloth. Dior prided himself on the handwork in his creations, especially when the craft generates formal possibility. Here, the stitches that anchor each pleat can actually be seen. Signs of artisanry, they are not obsessively hidden.

was the year of invention. It was sure and unequivocal. Dior invented the postwar disposition for amplitude of textile, creating a silhouette that, at its inception, applied drapery with the fullness of the Baroque to a preconceived and idealized armature of the human body. Dior's long life in the arts during the 1930s and 1940s had perhaps prepared him best for his exquisite proposition in fashion. He was offering a new aesthetic. Reflecting later, Dior himself would insist upon the political substance of his innovation, recalling that "The New Look . . . was a success only because it reflected the mood of the time—a mood that sought refuge from the mechanical and impersonal in a return to tradition and enduring values. . . . In an era as serious as ours, where national luxury means artillery and jet aircraft, we must defend every inch of our own personal luxury. . . . Our civilization is a luxury, and we are defending it." Luxury, manifest in opulent materials and, especially in 1947, in the privileged return of copious textile, permeates every Dior garment of that year.

Significantly, Dior made the bounty of material evident using the obvious contradiction between disciplined shaping and profligate drapery. He was creating a molded upper body tapering down to a caricaturelike corseted waist. Dresses and suits flare directly from the waist, enhancing its fabled tininess. With its dramatic burst of abundance, the engorged skirt sets off the narrow shoulders, the shaped and lifted bust, and the conelike tapering to the diminutive midriff. Dior demonstrated his mastery of pleats in the first collection: it was essential to be able to move subtly from the controlled use of fabric to the fullness that he favored in skirts, peplums, and in some cases even at the shoulder. Box pleats, knife pleats, and a virtuoso repertoire of dressmaking and pleating techniques allowed the compressed junctures of fabric to flow in wide release.

That first year, Dior immediately made fashion sensational again. War's necessary restrictions and a prevailing ethos of utilitarian clothing—there was even a classification in Great Britain called "utility" dress—had purposefully repudiated glamor. Dior wholeheartedly embraced the glamor and refinement of clothing down to the smallest details. Many suits and dresses in the 1947 collections, for example, buttoned at the back. Believing in the fashion of the past, Dior was thinking of a time of ladies' maids and the artistic ritual of dressing as much as he was of the finesse of displacing a function to a contrived place. Noting this predilection in the spring collection, *Harper's Bazaar* (May 1947) illustrated many garments front and back or, using what was to become a special strategy for witnessing the Dior silhouette, the side view, thus making it appear razor thin with extravagant extensions. Whether in front or in back, the buttons served as both a reminder of fashion's past and a means of showing the new structure. Hats added to the deliberate overall composition that Dior was formulating. Of

"Chérie" dinner dress, spring-summer 1947. Sapphire-blue changeant silk taffeta. Gift of Christian Dior, 1948 (CI 48.13 a,b)

"Chérie" exemplifies "The New Look" in all its salient elements: sloped shoulder, raised bustline, narrowed waist, and a monumental volume of skirt falling away from a padded hipline to below the calf. The New Look arrived uncompromised and complete, not as a tentative suggestion or stage in evolution. Here, the skirt is made of the full width of the fabric, selvage to selvage, disposed horizontally. Consequently, at the waist the necessary folding under of the pleated fullness creates a compressed, thirteen-and-one-half yard seam allowance, the substantial bulk of which pads the hips.

"Aladin" dinner dress, belted and unbelted, fall-winter 1947. Champagne silk satin. Gift of Bettina Ballard, 1958 (CI 58.50.1 a,b)

Dior loved the paradoxical juxtaposition of the ordinary and extraordinary. No garment more concisely and consummately represents his use of such contradiction than this one, which *Harper's Bazaar* immediately dubbed a "Mother Hubbard" dress in acknowledgment of its tentlike shape when unbelted. As Dior intended that it be worn belted, the essential Dior dialectic between the fullness of drapery and taut shaping to the body functions chiefly as a before-and-after phenomenon. Even when worn belted, where it comes into shape on the body, the dress retains the appearance of the broadest, least tailored construction. The designer's cognizance of fashion history may have afforded an eighteenth-century model, the mantua, for this combination of ample drapery secured to the body strategically and capable of being released. Further, in another *dix-huitième* touch, Dior introduced a coquettish aspect in the plunging décolletage.

the "Bar" suit (see page 21), *Harper's Bazaar* noted, "Balance for the silhouette—the wide, bowed hat-line." Dior's hats customarily frame the face but from the outset, they served chiefly to fulfill the silhouette, acting like large brims complementing the wide base of the long and full skirt. Other instances of accessories accent the richness of contour that Dior preferred; *Harper's Bazaar* described of a natural-linen coat, "Again he stresses the large-scale hat, and a big muff of leopard skin, effective against the pure monotone of linen."

While the American clients, except for evening, shied away from excessive décolletage, Dior, practicing his sculptural technique, was already carving away the upper chest even as he added structure at bust and waist. The 1947 "Aladin" dress (see pages 16 and 17) anticipated a variety of Dior shapes, including the deepest décolletage that seems to expose a portion of the breast. In fact, the achievement of The New Look and its implications for the next decade arrived in many ways born full-blown from the head of Christian Dior in 1947. Not only was the silhouette wholly reasoned, the means of achieving it were realized as well.

"Aladin" dinner dress, detail, fall-winter 1947. Champagne silk satin. Gift of Bettina Ballard, 1958 (CI 58.50.1 a,b). See also pages 16 and 17.

Although Dior's primary aesthetic reference for this dress is the eighteenth century, the fitted back bodice that cleaves to the body and the pattern piece that creates all the fullness in the unbelted front are allusions to the construction of 1880s–1890s at-home gowns. This detail suggests that, within the overall volume, there is the exact and rational dressmaking at which Dior excelled. Yet the effect is entirely one of legerdemain: Dior accomplished a magician's feat by disposing shape within the formless grandeur of massive drapery.

"Bar" suit. Jacket, spring-summer 1947. Beige silk shantung. Gift of Mrs. John Chambers Hughes, 1958 (CI 58.34.30). **Day skirt, executed in 1969 from a 1947 design.** Black wool. Gift of Christian Dior, 1969 (CI 69.40)

The relationship between designer and client is dynamic in the couture, often allowing for modified versions of the original design. Some of these are ultimately more or less sanctioned; others are ostracized and not publicly acknowledged by the House. Documents in the Dior archives demonstrate that the original version of the "Bar" suit employed a notched collar. This variation with a shawl collar, perhaps the result of a client's demand, was officially photographed by Dior at the time of its creation, indicating the imprimatur of the House of Dior.

Although Dior created many notched collars, he was a fervent advocate of shawl collars and curved necklines. Arguably, the shawl collar plays effectively with the curvaceous forms Dior articulated at the shoulders and hips. The notched lapel is more often found in the work of Adrian and other suit makers of the 1940s who stressed angled geometries.

"Mystère" day coat and center-front detail, fall-winter 1947. Black wool with moss-green silk taffeta trim. Gift of Irene Stone, in memory of her daughter, Mrs. Ethel S. Green, 1959 (CI 59.26.2)

Is the mystery in the black coat that of a shadowy seduction? Is the mystery in the revelation of an apparent interior, selectively revealed? Is the mystery in the shaping of an armature referential to and hyperbolic of the body that is clearly not anatomy itself? Dior knew the poetry of vestment, but he also knew the narrative possible in a garment.

One of the most typical ploys of Dior's design is the juxtaposition of modest and luxurious materials, which enhances the tactility of both. This detail is an example: a voluminous fan of green taffeta is inserted at the center-front skirt; layers of green taffeta are also visible at the neckline. Any observer would assume that there is a green dress within. The astonishment that resolves the mystery is that the coat is green and black, and whatever is worn within remains to be seen.

"Eugénie" ball gown and neckline detail, 1947. Pink Nylon lace. Gift of Mrs. Byron C. Foy, 1953 (CI 53.40.2 a-c)

Fashion history's equivalent of Impressionism is the silhouette of the Second Empire. At the matrix of the modern era, this style betokened the new. As both high culture and low culture have embraced Impressionism for its most salubrious, blithe aspects, so the court of Eugénie, familiar from F. X. Winterhalter's mid-nineteenth-century paintings, commands a continuing interest. The full circumference of this gown's sweeping bell shape disposed toward the back and its lacy sheerness recall the 1860s. Like Impressionism, the revival of the Second Empire can be a bottleneck causing banality and sentiment in its retro forms. Dior imparted incomparable luxury to the finish, suggesting that he was able to surpass what could easily be a stale icon by sheer extravagance.

A detail of lace at the scalloped strapless neckline reveals Dior's means of structure. Tiny curlicues of wire support the lace in the same way that the unseen bones support the bodice. In the small and the large form, Dior substantiated structure, even when the effect seems lacy and light.

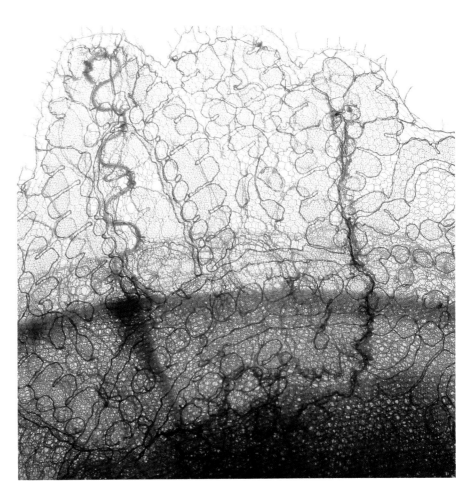

1948

"Diamant Noir" cocktail dress, detail, fall-winter 1948. Burgundy changeant silk taffeta. Courtesy Mrs. Janos Scholz. See also page 40.

Ever seeking the harmonious fusion of a structured form with a fluidity of fabric and the appearance of loose amplitude, Dior developed a formula that sets up the armature and then floats fabric barely anchored to the structure. A detail of the skirt of a cocktail dress shows Dior's approach to design: he attached the textile very loosely over a more rigid support. In this case, silk taffeta, which has a crisp body, is puffed and gathered over a more simply cut and stiffened understructure. Each puff is held in place by only one basting stitch.

is the year when the supposed "new" that was initiated in 1947 was challenged to proceed. As "The New Look" fixed itself as name to Dior's enterprise, each collection promised a newer impression under a rubric that had to justify and celebrate the change. Moreover, what had been an achievement in the context of disarray and moderate expectations in 1947 was, a year later, the most-watched spectacle of the fashion world. Dior had in the space of one year reestablished Paris as the heart of fashion innovation and quality. The designer's optimism and opulence were being rewarded by widespread esteem and popularity.

Dior was soaring in 1948. He called his spring collection "Envol," signifying flight. Skirts rose with the easy lift of a postwar clipper aircraft, often creating an effect very like a bustle. To those who thought Dior ludicrous and criticized his work as historicist souvenirs and imprisoned bodies, the spring 1948 collection reinforced the constrained body and the New Look silhouette. Long skirts were shrouded in pontoons of stiffened cloth, often seeming more to benefit the camera's eye than the client's ease in sitting. But examples such as the "Drag" afternoon dress (see page 30) demonstrate that Dior was both formal and informal in his style: he allowed a bunching of fabrics as if he were dealing with pure drapery, but he always adhered to the substructure that recalls the New Look silhouette.

Invariably, Dior's insistence on a new name and declaration

Dress, 1948. Red silk twill. Gift of
Elizabeth Nimmich Saunders, 1992
(1992.171 a–d)

Beginning with his 1947 New Look collection, Dior always included at least one
shirtwaist-style dress. The designer had a
capacity to see fashion history through the
mirror of fashion plates and engravings,
and Charles Dana Gibson's heroic turn-of-
the-century prints were the inspiration for
a more intricate version of the shirtlike
blouse, the mundane shirtwaist dress.

This Dior leitmotif further suggests his
willingness to work with an established
form but to complicate its construction
and render it idiosyncratic. This shirtwaist reads as a full dress. But, in fact, it
is constructed similarly to Dior's ball
gowns of the period, with a separate
bodice and skirt and a belt that hides the
waist seam. Dior's more complex resolution does have an effect on the appearance, however, assuring a more perfect fit
and allowing the waist to be more severely
constrained.

of style was mitigated by his return to favored motifs. In spring 1948, there were many dresses that could easily be confused with those of the year before. Dior did not disclaim his own preoccupations, even as he did proclaim a fresh title for each collection.

If a swag of cloth, inspired by the Second Empire, animated the spring 1948 collection, cloth whipped back and forth in the fall 1948 collection, known as the "Zig Zag." A draftsman's swift and knowing hand appears to have inspired Dior to a like tour de force of nonchalant asymmetry, swooping hemlines, and a feeling of agitation. This windblown collection possessed the energy to torque collars and décolletage and to flutter High Gothic cuff finials. It was, of course, Dior's innate sense of poetry that prompted such a collection for a fall season. Yet in other instances in 1948, such as the "Poulette" dinner dress (see page 39), the crisscrossing lines of force rest with greater stability on the body, in no way unmooring the effects of Second Empire remembrance. Dior's second step was to invigorate the statuesque and doll-like poise of "The New Look" with the energy of twisted and folded cloth. The year was not a disavowal of the last collection. It was, rather, an animation of its form. The doll came to life.

"Drag" afternoon dress, spring-summer 1948. Navy-blue wool. Gift of Dorothy Cox, 1968 (CI 68.82 a.b)

Dior was particularly adept at modernizing historical garments. Here, he emulated the draped apronlike swag of 1880s dresses but anchored it with one large decorative button. The modernity of the dress prevails in the utmost simplicity and economy of cut of its torso-cleaving bodice. Dior sutured the extreme body consciousness of the top to the asymmetrically gathered fullness of the skirt. The donor, on giving the dress to The Costume Institute in 1968, referred to its "'riding habit' skirt."

Day suit, spring-summer 1948. Navy-blue wool. Gift of Mrs. Byron C. Foy, 1953 (CI 53.40.18 a,b)

To look at a Dior day suit from a back view is like observing historic premodern costume. This view suggests the way Dior cut to the body as it had been reconfigured by his wasp-waisted corset. The small-ness of the waist is clearly exaggerated by the presence of padding at the hipline of the skirt as well as batting interfacings in the skirt/peplum of the jacket.

A seventeenth-century silhouette is markedly similar. The natural shoulder and voluptuous hipline repudiate most women's suits of the 1940s. For the majority of designers of this time, the suit was widest at the padded shoulder, tapered only gradually at the waist, and skimmed the tightly girdled haunches, suggesting a longer line into the skirt. Dior deliberately avoided and subverted the convention to create a suit with his own distinctive and curvilinear line.

**Day coat and back-shoulder detail,
1948.** Black wool with sky-blue broadcloth trim. Gift of Mrs. Phyllis B.
Lambert, 1954 (CI 54.6.7 a,b)

Varying a typical redingote, Dior inserted
the fluid and flexible into the robust coat.
Even in his strictest tailoring, Dior frequently introduced the supple draping
fabric he loved. In this case, the flyaway
shoulder yoke is a continuous piece,
extending the back of the sleeve to form
a large soft welt-tuck.

    In a couture capability not possible in
a less exacting ready-to-wear garment,
Dior employed a clean insertion of contrasting fabrics at collar and cuffs.

"Abandon" afternoon dress, fall-winter 1948. Black silk faille. Gift of Bettina Ballard, 1958 (CI 58.7.8 a,b)

Vogue (September 15, 1948) noted the extraordinary neckline of this dress, specifying the "plunging neckline with side-slanted fold." The asymmetrical gathering of fabric swoops around the neck in the same manner of the 1948 skirts but closes low in the front, opening an expanse of shoulder and poitrine and perhaps even suggesting more in its seductive gyration. Dior consistently liked scarflike effects to frame a very nude shoulderline. Here, he did not have to place linen or other materials in the décolletage: he simply used the natural bunching of silk to serve as an adjustable "modesty" for the deeply plunging neckline.

"Poulette" dinner dress, spring-summer 1948. Black silk faille. Gift of Irene Stone, in memory of her daughter, Mrs. Ethel S. Greene, 1959 (CI 59.26.1 a-c)

The zigzag folding effect of the dress's skirt creates an 1860s triangulated silhouette. The restrained buttoned blouse-jacket top is in dramatic contrast to the voluminous skirt. Not even a collar inflects the jacketlike bodice, thus calling more attention to the ankle-length skirt with its zigzag overdrape.

Although Dior often constructed his bodices and skirts as independent elements, they were always visually integrated. In "Poulette," the folded pattern piece of the skirt diminishes at the hipline to form a peplumlike effect: what appears to be a continuation of the bodice is, in fact, an integral part of the skirt.

"Diamant Noir" cocktail dress, fall-winter 1948. Burgundy changeant silk taffeta. Courtesy Mrs. Janos Scholz.

Harper's Bazaar (November 1948) described the season's "Lampshade dress" as "a brand-new silhouette." Of course, Dior took advantage of taffeta's ability to puff and crinkle, and the magazine noted that the material's "airy parachute texture blows easily into the proper drapings and flouncings and puffings." The swords-into-plowshares allusion adumbrates the postwar context in which Dior's dream-like luxury flourished.

1949

"Ficelle" day dress, detail, spring-summer 1949. Natural linen with allover silk passementerie trim. Gift of Mrs. Byron C. Foy, 1955 (CI 55.76.1 a-c). See also page 53.

That Dior relished the friction between opposites is nowhere more prevalent than in the combination of a mundane material and an uncommon treatment, a dialectic equivalent to Claude Lévi-Strauss's contrast of the raw and the cooked. Silk passementerie, indicative of the civilizing element, is anchored against matte natural linen, suggestive of fundamental dress. The intricately curled spirals evoke flowers; within the whirls, three-dimensional grapes are created in the manner of stumpwork, a traditional fashion ornamentation.

brought the name "Trompe l'Oeil," a motif that had long been present in Dior's sensibility. The elegant ambiguity that had characterized inner-outer, autonomous-contingent elements marked the spring 1949 collection with a particular intensity. Collars doubled, the paths of materials reversed, and shapes and proportions seemed to morph. The fall 1949-50 "Mid-Century" collection arrived with a nondescriptive title that signaled the continuing evolution of the ideas of the "Trompe l'Oeil" collection. The name "Mid-Century" did not describe the practice of complication that had continued into fall. Likewise, Dior's lifelong fascination with the button for both closure and effect was of exceptional importance in this year.

Thus, the "Moulin à Vent" cocktail dress (see page 57) is indicative of 1949. Yet, arguably, even in such successes of a material kind, Dior was preeminently a painter and draftsman, not a sculptor. The three-dimensionality of fashion on the body and especially the defined exoskeleton that Dior created might lead one to believe that this fashion designer was a sculptor manqué. Rather, he was a renderer manqué, delighting in fabric as the illustrator might enjoy the crumble of conté or the painter might prize the scumble of pigment. In 1949, Dior acknowledged more than ever the suave drawing and deft deceptions that he admired. Friend to Christian Bérard, René Gruau, Jean Cocteau, and other Paris illustrator-artists going back to his days as an art dealer, Dior expressed himself as an artist at mid-century.

Further, when Dior's linear fervor was not paramount in 1949, his love of surface effect was. In both day dresses and evening wear, Dior triumphed that year by his uses of the most extravagant embroideries and swarming surface effects. If the principal intent of trompe l'oeil for Dior was artistic license and the emulation of art, the secondary was the emphasis on surface. In order for trompe l'oeil to work, the eye must be intrigued by the surface and aware that such a skin is superficial not blandly but grandly. Rebé embroidery and other dazzling effects of the surface came to the fore in 1949: the result is that an artist's illusions cohabit with an artisan's techniques.

Eliding both art and technique in illusionary deceit, Dior manipulated pockets in 1949. In the spring, breast pockets were used to augment the bust. In the fall, the "Dali" dinner dress (see page 61) exemplified Dior playing with pockets and flaps at the bust to ascribe it more volume. Such details recall the ingenious pockets of Elsa Schiaparelli, especially those of the late 1930s. Schiaparelli was also a master of trompe l'oeil and a partisan of artists and artistic collaboration in apparel; in her "Desk Suit" (1936) and in other tailoring as well, she had focused on pockets, functional and decorative, for structure and for enhancement of the silhouette.

At the same time, Dior was becoming canonical in the world of style. His collections were received as pronouncements of fashion direction, more oracular than speculative. His work in 1949 was in pursuit of his own abiding themes; this was not a year of radical change, but instead one of reinforcement of the designer's personal vision. At mid-century, Dior resolved to do more and to do the same better.

"Pactole" cocktail dress, fall-winter 1949. Gold silk satin. Gift of Mrs. Byron C. Foy, 1953 (CI 53.40.36 a-c)

Dior realized the natural contradiction between a basic dress form and a radiant luxury-implying material. The same design could easily result in the most jejune day dress. Luxurious heavyweight gold silk makes a Rumpelstiltskin fantasy out of the ordinary. By 1949, Dior was challenging, albeit with his perfect sense of the prettiest etiquette and protocol, the fixed elements of dress. To transpose elements of dress—male to female, day to cocktail—constituted a polite revolution and a means of being modern within Dior's resolutely historicist canon.

Day dress, 1949. Navy-blue wool with white cotton piqué trim. Gift of Despina Messinesi, 1978 (1978.40.2 a-d)

Dior's 1947 New Look collection made him what many, whether admiringly or enviously, called the dictator of fashion. Surely he was able to command style. But Dior's fashion was perhaps less sovereign than some have imagined. This day dress offers separate collars and cuffs that can be either buttoned on or omitted. Two Diorisms are notable. He used the button accents to suggest a decorative placket, and he extended the surplice neckline toward the left hip, his traditional point of resolution. With these gestures, Dior added an implied decorative vocabulary for the navy buttons and also extended line as deftly as a Brancusi sculpture does.

Such is Dior's navy-blue equivalent of the Chanel little black dress. He, too, rendered a most traditional dress, resembling that of a servant, into a transcendent garment by means of both finesse and the subtle, but notable, increment of design intentionality.

Dinner dress and skirt detail, 1949.
Black wool. Gift of Mrs. Byron C. Foy,
1953 (CI 53.40.40 a-d)

A tour de force of construction, this seemingly simple dinner dress reveals a construction that appears to be composed of four panels of fabric buttoning at the shoulder and falling to form a sheath. In fact, there are multiple pattern pieces, and the dress, once again illustrating a Dior characteristic, is seamed at the waist. A sophistication resides in the willingness to sublimate all the complication into the design and let the spectator read the dress as effortlessly simple. At the same time, Dior's couture sculpting to the individual client depends upon the intricate pattern pieces and could not have been accomplished if he were working with the larger geometries that seem to create the garment.

Unlike Chanel, who prided herself on a buttonhole for every button, Dior prized the allusive aspects of decoration; thus, the nonfunctional buttons at the hem. Moreover, a pleat at the front hem conceals a line of seven nonfunctional buttons that are revealed with each step or in sitting. The zipper closing is hidden at side-front under the panel. Dior's consistent preference was for the genteel illusion and the pretty play of decoration, even when it served no functional purpose.

Hat, 1949. Black felt. Purchase, Friends
of The Costume Institute, 1978
(1978.281.4)

Souvenirs of Dior's earlier career as an art
dealer are found in his hats conceived as
sculptures. In this example, Dior may have
been re-creating a bicorne or a regional
headdress, but as an adaptation of a broad
horizontal to be perched on the head and
subject to personal adjustment. The ends
of the hat can be either curled or flattened.
As decisive as Dior was about dress, his
hats allowed for individual interpretation
and, sometimes, metamorphosis.

"Ficelle" day dress, spring-summer 1949. Natural linen with allover silk passementerie trim. Gift of Mrs. Byron C. Foy, 1955 (CI 55.76.1 a-c)

The center-front button closure continues beyond its actual function to become a provocation, implying perpetual unbuttoning. The décolletage thus created mediates the proper and the seductive. The button-and-loop form used here is a practical resolution that retains its allusion to the decorative curlicues and knots of the complex surface embroidery.

The components of embroidery suggest the extraordinary range of resources available to the couture. Silk floss, rat tail, and silk-floss corded rat tail animate the austere canvas of linen. Self-fabric "grapes" lend a further dimensionality and reiterate the ball button closure.

"Pisanelle" ensemble and collar details, fall-winter 1949. Navy-blue silk velvet and satin. Gift of Mrs. Byron C. Foy, 1953 (CI 53.40.9 a-c)

"There is," art historian James Beck has said, "a subtlety of interpretation coupled with a confident elegance that makes Pisanello one of the most widely appreciated painters of the first generation [of Italian Renaissance artists]." Dior aptly admired Antonio Pisanello (ca. 1395– ca. 1455) for his refined attention to detail and his fascination with clothing materials; the painter often represented complicated fabrics and clothing treatments in his frescoes and in obsessive details in his drawings. In this ensemble, the skirt plays on matte and shiny surfaces to create a sense of the waist-sash as trompe-l'oeil bow and gores of the skirt as streamers. Pisanello saw the plaiting of an angel's wing or the materials of Renaissance *Gesamtkunstwerk* noble attire in a like manner.

Both of the details pictured may be indebted to Italian Renaissance costume as articulated by Pisanello. The detail on the left shows how the collar forms a wide capelike effect and how the volume of the sleeve ends not in a cuff but in a box-pleat edge. The detail on the right reveals the construction of the collar ending as an anchored wing, splaying back like a kimono sleeve with the insertion underneath of a Western melon-shaped sleeve. In Pisanello's Sant'Anastasia fresco, there are garments of a similar effect. The painter's world of Venice, Verona, Rome, Milan, and Ferrara put him in contact with both Eastern and Western dress.

"Moulin à Vent" cocktail dress and detail, fall-winter 1949. Black wool flannel and silk moiré. Gift of Doris Hakim, 1974 (1974.312.1 a-c)

Harper's Bazaar (October 1949) described this "windmill" ensemble as "the best cocktail-dinner dress in the Dior collection and the best example of his new scissors movement. In black wool, it has an off-the-shoulder collar of moiré and a pair of moiré scissors at the side." The detail shows the zipper closure angling across the hipline in the manner of the bands of moiré giving energy equal to a wind-driven gust to every aspect of the dress. Anticipating his preoccupation with the man's tuxedo modified to womenswear,

Dior here played with the black textures, suggesting inner and outer, fundamental and incremental, working together in synergy.

Anchoring a major construction or decoration at the left hipline is a preferred Dior strategy. In this case, the arcs of moiré form an X over the left hipline. Dior introduced motion not merely to the skirt but to the bodice as well. Another Diorism, a considerable and daring décolletage, is made especially dynamic and beguiling by its degree of thrust. Dior was ever polite, but he provoked us to think of the dress as if in nonchalant flyaway suspension, and he just barely brought it back to the propriety he knew so well.

Calot hat, 1949. Black velour with ermine tails. Gift of Mrs. Byron C. Foy, 1955 (CI 55.76.36)

Late-day and cocktail dresses engaged Dior's imagination intensely; their accompanying hats exemplify Dior's great achievement in fusing the ordinary and the extraordinary. Dior anointed the shape of this small head-hugging cap with imperial gesture by ornamenting it with a cluster of ermine tails.

Cartwheel hat, 1949. Black straw and feathers. Gift of the Family of Mrs. M. Lincoln Shuster, 1977 (1977.363.10)

Dior defined the body with a narrow waist and expansive bell-shaped skirt, like those of Second Empire dress. He created overall equilibrium by topping the figure with a broad-brimmed hat. These vast cartwheels act as counterbalances to Dior's big skirts. Additionally, Dior's hats enjoyed the same textural delight as his suits and dresses. In this instance, a perimeter band of feathers creates a continuous lash that flickers light and dark across the face.

"Dali" dinner dress and bodice details, fall-winter 1949. Gold-and-black silk brocade. Gift of Mr. and Mrs. Henry Rogers Benjamin, 1965 (CI 65.14.2 a-c)

Dior's lifetime interest in art is manifest in this simulation of the work of Salvador Dali. Two folds, exaggerated pocket flaps draped over the bustline, suggest a little vest and establish the escapade and masquerade of Dali's illusionism. Dior's corseted silhouette emphasizes the bust stance, but here he has obliterated that artifice by his use of the vestlike layer. In fact, Dali's actual fashion collaboration with Schiaparelli was more physical and macabre. Dior's version of Dali is cerebral and in tune with the designer's own penchant for dresses that play with bareness and covering.

Beyond its initial reference to nature, the leaf pattern is very un-Dali. Dior has chosen to disregard Dali's interest in eccentric and Surrealist textiles. It is characteristic of Dior to see an affinity through one detail, ignoring many differences. By the late 1940s, Dali was a démodé artist, disavowed by the Surrealists and alien to the popular taste.

Dior employed an elaborate piecing of fabric to create the proper shaping for the part of the bodice that adheres to the body. The harmony Dior established between the paradox of a rigidly and artificially sculpted torso and an emancipated flow of ample skirt material is one that, in conceptual terms, might have attracted Dali. But Dali's impish impoliteness certainly would have been offensive to Dior. The clever artist and the courtly fashion designer had known each other probably from art circles in Paris in the 1930s, and the acquaintance continued until Dior's death. They worked together on the decor of the 1951 de Beistégui ball at the Palazzo Labia in Venice.

**"Gruau" evening dress, fall-winter
1949.** Blue silk satin. Gift of Mrs. A.
Moore Montgomery, 1957 (CI 57.55 a,b)

Dior superimposed a button-down propriety with exuberant twists of heavily
gathered satin. The apparent spiraling
of the gown's angled forms obliterates
the designer's resolute dependence on
parts: heavily boned bodice and wasp-
waisted skirt.

The asymmetrical sweep and juxtaposition of tailored effects with dramatic
accents of drapery allude to the gestural
drawings of René Gruau (b. 1909).
Gruau's bold and reductive illustrations
seize detail and movement. The illustrator's
finest work was for Dior. Correspondingly,
a great evening dress was dedicated to
Gruau.

Dinner dress, fall-winter 1949. Black wool and silk faille. Gift of Rosamond Bernier, 1989 (1989.130.1 a,b)

Those quick to characterize and vilify Dior as the maker of the eternally and oppressively feminine for the 1940s and 1950s must find his leitmotif of menswear adaptation cautionary. He appropriated gray-flannel tailoring, houndstooth, white cotton piqué, and other elements of menswear. One of Dior's great achievements was to create from the vocabulary of men's tuxedos. Here, a black wool column is accented with black silk faille that would be in a man's tuxedo lapel and cummerbund. Visible in the asymmetrical wrapping of the pattern pieces is his interest in the drape of fabric.

"Cygne Noir" ball gown, fall-winter 1949–50. Black silk satin and velvet. Gift of Doris Hakim. 1974 (1974.312.2 a,b)

Dior recounted of dress names, "According to the charming old tradition of the Paris Couture, the model gets a name instead of a number. I christen it 'Rascal.' 'Darling.' or 'Sardanapalus.' A chosen theme, the circumstances of its creation, a chance happening, a superstitious idea, and particularly the impression made by the dress itself can all be responsible for the name. No matter how uninspired it is, nobody ever forgets the name after it is once given." Dior's appellation "black swan" for an elegantly flaring shape—which, as in "Pisanelle" (see page 54), incorporates matte and shiny as complements—is inspired.

"Junon" ball gown, fall-winter 1949.
Pale-blue cotton net with iridescent
sequin embroidery. Gift of Mrs.
Byron C. Foy, 1953 (CI 53.40.5 a-d)

The peacock, sacred to Juno, provides the
reference for Dior's gown. The Rebé
embroidery, of exceptional richness,
allows the soft platelets of tiered fabrics
to function as if they were the overlap-
ping feathers of the peacock's tail. Of all
Dior's works of the 1940s, the "Venus"
(see page 70) and "Junon" ball gowns
most fully represent his reliance on opulence to reestablish traditional values.
Even in the inevitable comparison to
nineteenth-century dress, it would be
hard to think of a garment equal in luxu-
riance. Of course, Dior complemented his
old-style grandeur with the modern touch
of the strapless neckline, itself made possible by the traditional construction of
the bodice.

"Venus" ball gown, fall-winter 1949.
Gray silk net with opalescent sequin
embroidery. Gift of Mrs. Byron C. Foy,
1954 (CI 53.40.7 a-e)

Amidst the silvery spumelike net resembling sea foam, pearlescent shell-shaped
scallops pronounce Venus risen from the
waters. But Dior has not only evoked the
story of Venus: he has also created an
ideal of beauty. The sparkling splendor of
such a garment is the dream of a ball
gown. For Dior, fantasy was both mar-
velous and ideal. He strove to make an
archetypal evening gown, but he was also
creating the confections for the great
postwar theme balls.

1950

"Scarlatti" ball gown, detail, spring-summer 1950. Pink silk ribbon and white cotton-lace ruffles. Gift of Elizabeth Fairall, 1950 (CI 50.78 a-c). See also page 75.

Gowns named by Dior after composers share an unabashed femininity. Fragile chiffons swooped into silk rose-anchored bustles, sheer organzas layered and petaled into giant blooms, and lace gathered into tiered Winterhalter confections were called "Offenbach," "Poulenc," and "Schumann." Though the effects were often operatic, Dior's details are invariably leggiero.

The spirals of ribbon and lace of the "Scarlatti" ball gown are hand applied along one edge so that they stand semi-upright in relief rather than flat.

suggested to Dior the names "Vertical" for spring and "Oblique" for fall, titles that brought the collections under the thrall of lines and angles. Once again, for all their ostensible newness, the collections of 1950 pursued 1949's involution and sweetness in their uses of illusions. In particular, the collars of daywear tended to grow larger in 1950, and collars and necklines were still the place where Dior offered an amplitude of materials with magical draping and folding. The ambiguities and ironies of preceding years simply grew in scale and ambition.

If there was one particularly great illusion in Dior's work in 1950, it was that he devoted attention to the grand geometry of his clothing, perhaps in keeping with art's widespread tendency toward abstraction at that time. But Dior was steadfastly the purveyor of little pleasures and infinitesimal illusions. Thus, the dense decoration on some of his gowns named after composers vacillates between abstract and natural forms. Daywear in 1950 depended more than ever on the hidden possibilities of form; our "Trompette" day dress (see page 76) betokens a simple engineering that results in easier mobility.

One dialectic seemed especially persuasive in 1950: the adapted masculine and the unabashed feminine. Some daywear could constitute a substantial engineering given to robust fabrications that come out of the tradition of menswear, but evening gowns invariably stressed the wholly delicate and vulnerable. After

1950, this trait of using the vocabulary of menswear for day and offering the utmost in feminine delicacy for evening persisted in Dior's work as a tacit manner of thinking. Of the many ways in which Dior's attainment and sensibility seem pertinent years later, this dichotomy within his sensibility is among the most important. Designers of the 1970s through the 1990s have "discovered" again what Dior institutionalized in his thinking in 1950.

The music-referenced dresses by Dior suggest his interest in an old-fashioned synesthesia; he genuinely believed in the correlations among the arts. His was a seamless cultural world of music, art, and dress. For Dior and other couturiers of the 1950s, the assumption could rightly be made that the clients were equally sophisticated and involved in the arts.

"Scarlatti" ball gown, spring-summer 1950. Pink silk ribbon and white cotton-lace ruffles. Gift of Elizabeth Fairall, 1950 (CI 50.78 a-c)

Dior named a number of gowns after composers and operas. These are among his most flamboyant works. It is not known for certain if this dress was named for Alessandro or Domenico Scarlatti, though its rococo repetitions and resplendence may allude to Domenico. Whirls of white lace and pink silk ribbon embroidery extend into huge scalloped forms that undulate with controlled regularity at the hemline. This dress with a train, continuing the scalloping onto the horizontal of the floor, also demonstrates Dior's historical and ceremonial associations with music. As music can transport us back to the eighteenth century, so too can the courtlike elegance of a modern dress convey an evocative sense of history.

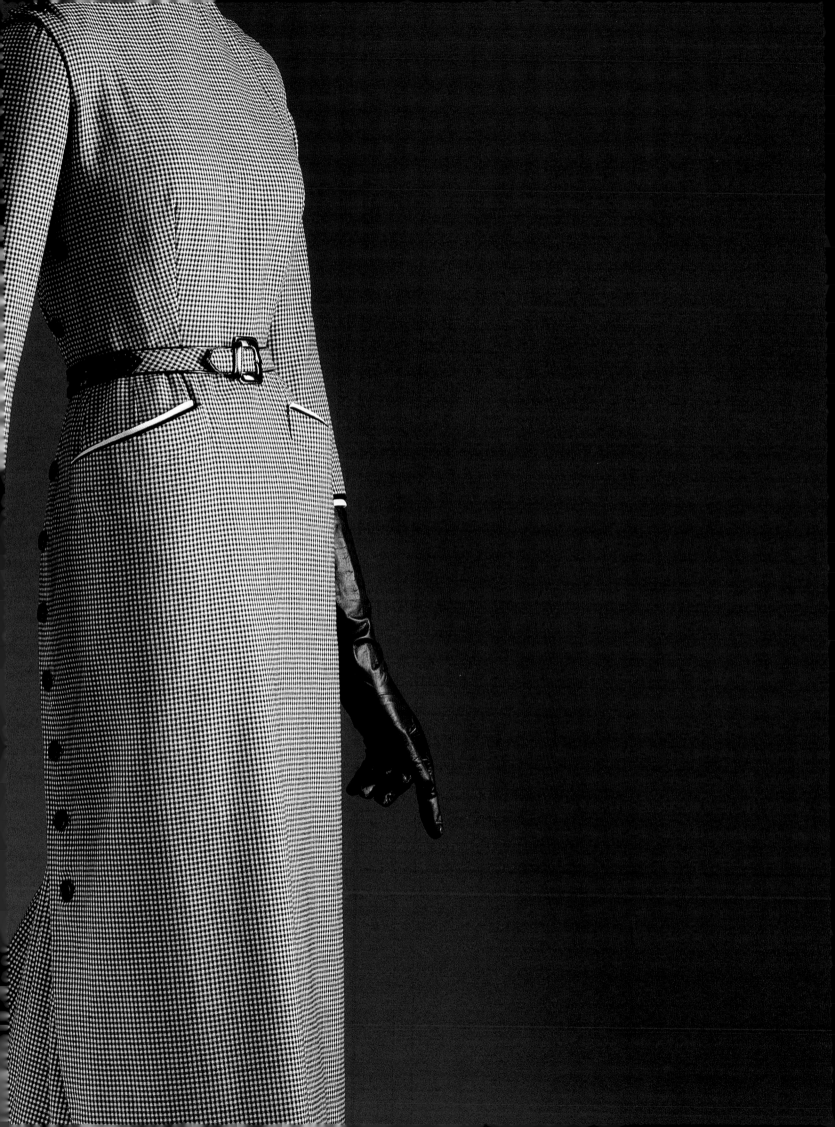

"Trompette" day dress and skirt detail, spring-summer 1950. Black-and-white checked wool with black silk velvet and white cotton piqué trim. Gift of Mrs. Phyllis B. Lambert, 1954 (CI 54.6.3 a-c)

Dior combined a narrow silhouette with a trumpet skirt. The title suggests three aspects: synesthesia in its reference to music, silhouette in its allusion to the shape of a trumpet, and the annunciatory pride inferred by "trumpeting."

Dior's narrow skirts typically accommodate walking by means of a hidden fullness below the knee. In this case, he utilized that amplitude as a visible design feature.

The minicheck suggests the safety and conservatism of menswear but inflected by the fact that the skirt's patterning is slashed vertically with the grain and expanded by vertical fan-shaped inserts. The buttoning of parts refers to the layered propriety of a man's three-piece suit as well.

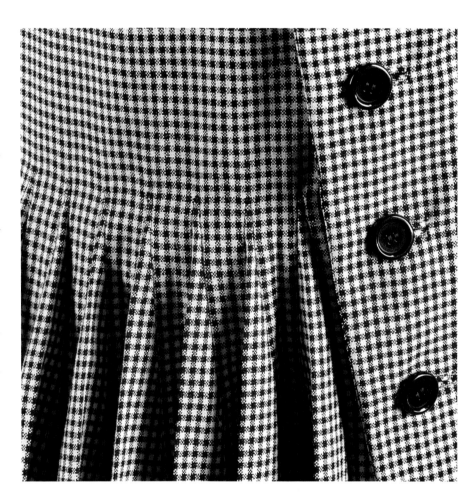

Melon cap, 1950. Black velour and felt. Gift of Mary S. Ryan. 1981 (1981.151.11)

Dior rarely imposed his sense of humor on his designs. This hat with a touch of whimsy may be less about the designer's wit than it is about his reserve: he insists on a hat so simple in its architectural presence that any viewer has to decide between its potential drollery and its more likely severity.

Hat, 1950. Dark-tan fur felt. Gift of Mrs. Charlotte R. Gutman, 1957 (CI 57.63.2)

Dior's affinity for the Second Empire is again evident here. The petite, perched hats of that period could be worn with both day wear and walking dresses. The faintly peculiar shapes, though generally symmetrical, could be pulled forward on a center-parted hairline or canted to the side. Dior's versions of these hats likewise depended on the topography and architectonics of 1950s hairstyles.

Dress and shoulder detail, fall-winter 1950. Black wool. Gift of Mrs. Byron C. Foy, 1953 (CI 53.40.16 a-d)

A simple tailor's construction turns out to be a virtuosity of the draper. What seems to be the revers of a wool dress is really a continuous piece of fabric that rolls back on itself. The fitted body of the bodice is modified by the double layer of fabric over the bustline. Dior's affinity for the folding and supple character of cloth modifies the potential austerity of the tailor's craft.

As seen in the detail above, the double layering of fabric across the chest, by augmenting the poitrine, in essence balances the proportions of the broad-hipped, voluptuous silhouette that he advocated.

1951

"Diorama" evening gown, detail, spring-summer 1951. Black silk mousseline and horsehair braid. Gift of Mrs. Byron C. Foy, 1953 (CI 53.40.13 a-c). See also page 97.

Dior understood the privileges of the couture. The structure of his suits and dresses trained their wearers in etiquette and carriage, and their visible signs of handicraft confirmed the couture's unique and time-honored capabilities. In even the most sophisticated design, Dior prized the touches of artisanry possible in the couture. One can see the stitch marks that anchor the separate horsehair ribbons to the mousseline.

was a year of resolution for Dior. His spring collection was dubbed "Oval," and the fall collection that Dior named the "Long Line" was more customarily called "Princesse" by the press and clients. Dior later referred to the fall 1951 collection as his favorite from among all others. Paradoxically, it was the collection that most defied the predictable aspect of Dior, raising the waist and seeking the extended line of the princess seams that would flow continuously from the top of the dress to the hem. He who had conceived the most horizontally segregated body of mid-century fashion was suddenly thinking in terms of a unified, uninflected vertical line.

The "Diorama" evening gown (see page 97), to which the designer attached his own name, identifies the initiative of 1951. Dior formulated a bell-shaped skirt slightly raised at the waist in order to achieve a longer line. But the grand silhouette is rendered sheer and supple by the extraction of horsehair braid from an inner structure to the linear and pliant exterior of the dress. Perhaps the Second Empire is the paradigm of the shape, but what the Second Empire hid, Dior disclosed, bringing all the structure palpably to the surface in the manner of a modern architect. Moreover, the horsehair, by enabling permissive ripples, is not merely a structural material but also a richly movemented line that was to articulate the long line to follow in the subsequent season. Even the tapering ends of the horsehair emulate princess seams;

 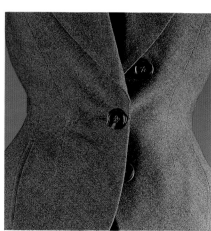

"Désirée" day suit and jacket details, spring-summer 1951. Gray wool. Gift of Janet A. Sloane, 1982 (1982.427.2 a,b)

By 1951, Dior had established his principle of adapting menswear to women's apparel using supremely feminine tailoring. This gray wool suit, an archetype of male attire, was flatteringly body conscious when interpreted by Dior. His dressmaking knowledge is evident in the rounded-shoulder and seamed-sleeve construction and also in the carved waistline of the jacket—all the couture dressmaker's extrapolations from men's tailoring. Two vestigial buttons, purely ornamental, bracket the one functional button at center-front.

Later in the 1950s, Sloan Wilson would tellingly describe the character of American postwar life in the novel *The Man in the Gray Flannel Suit* (1955), but Dior had already transfigured the suit into a woman's version. For Wilson, the gray suit was a straitjacket of conformity; for Dior, it was a matrix of creative invention. Thus, the designer of the utmost feminine silhouette used the defining materials of masculinity in a Diorism of masculine-feminine that abides in his work and is perpetuated and extended in the work of designers today.

"Partie Fine" cocktail dress and shoulder detail, spring-summer 1951.
Pleated, cream-colored silk shantung.
Gift of Mrs. Byron C. Foy, 1953
(CI 53.40.21 a-c)

What appears to be a one-piece dress is actually a separate bodice and skirt in Dior's underplayed and demanding design. The bodice has a boned corselet over which the pleated fabric has been anchored in the Diorism of a stiffened armature with floating, barely affixed pleated panels. The collar is held away from the neck by a line of hidden wire. Pink roses with green leaves were placed where Dior typically resolved the flow of the bodice: at the left side of the waist.

A detail of the shoulder suggests the way Dior has draped, rather than tailored, his forms, wrapping and tacking instead of cutting and piecing. The soft plaiting at neck and shoulder may allude—considering Dior's historical admiration and imagination—to eighteenth-century fichus that defined décolletage with softly gathered fabric.

they are released from mere stuctural obligation to stir the surface of the monumental dome silhouette.

It was in 1951 that Dior detached his subtle surfaces from the grand silhouette. It was his finest achievement of that year. He had always known and demonstrated, in his cocktail and evening dresses, that the skin of the garment was pliant and could be lifted away from a substructure, but in 1951 that principle became the prime focus of the collections.

"Quiproquo" cocktail dress, spring-summer 1951. Black-and-white printed silk twill with black silk-velvet trim. Gift of Mrs. Byron C. Foy, 1953 (CI 53.40.38 a-d)

In a dress unusual for Dior, Japanese characters are printed in black on a white ground. A separate black underbodicelike corselet gives the bodice a rigid support over which the softer draped overbodice is buttoned. Focus is given to the low curved neckline as in the manner of eighteenth-century dresses. Dior's avowal of the European past is paramount. In this instance, the use of a Japanism in the form of Japanese script presented in poetic form is wholly superficial; the thinking is Western. This textile was originally shown as another model in the same collection, "Grimoire." Presumably it was only at the initiative of the client that Dior created this slightly complicated version of "Quiproquo" from the fabric of the other dress.

Dinner dress and detail, fall-winter 1951. Bronze silk satin with allover black-bead and sequin embroidery. Gift of Mrs. Byron C. Foy, 1955 (CI 55.76.11)

In this Diorism, in which one layer is cut seductively low only to be filled in with another construction, a cutaway neckline reveals the contrasting underbodice. The detail shows the graduated beading in a houndstooth check—an allusion to menswear patterning transformed by an opulent womenswear technique.

"Sylvie" evening ensemble and sleeve detail, spring-summer 1951. Black silk taffeta. Gift of Mrs. Byron C. Foy. 1953 (CI 53.40.24 a-d)

Dior frequently paired his strapless, halter, or in other ways very revealing dresses with evening jackets and coats. A simple and narrow underdress is hidden under a voluminous taffeta coat. The fashion designer may have been sovereign, but this balance between disclosing and covering was, in such instances, determined by the client.

The detail of the sleeve points out how the fabric is gathered into a doughnut shape with a separate knot at the cap and then stitched onto the arm's eye. The effect is to distinguish clearly between this ring of bunched fabric and the shoulder and to form a powerful bicep-like mass above the bust.

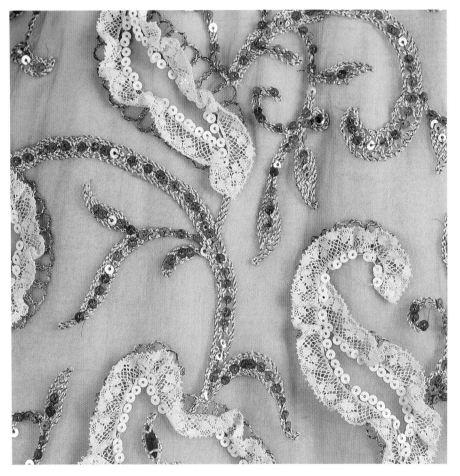

**"Comédie Légère" dinner dress and
detail, 1951.** Gray silk organza with
lace, sequin, and rhinestone embroidery.
Gift of Mrs. Byron C. Foy, 1953
(CI 53.40.37 a-c)

Dior chose touchstone adornments from
the well-established vocabulary of
Western dress and textiles. A combination
of paisley and foliate shapes is given a
rococo refinement with elaborate embroidery in the Dior taste, classic but hinting
at the exotic.

What reads from the front as a narrow
dress has a great deal of fullness concen-
trated in the back. Dior's complementing
use of the compact and the replete is generally present in the bodice vis-à-vis the
skirt. In the early 1950s, the influence of
the 1880s bustle gown was most profound
on Dior's evening gowns, and he brought
that period's manipulation of silhouette
of small and large to the front and side
views of a dress.

"Diorama" evening gown, spring-summer 1951. Black silk mousseline and horsehair braid. Gift of Mrs. Byron C. Foy, 1953 (CI 53.40.13 a-c)

It is characteristic of Dior to use the structural element horsehair as a decorative one. Attention is drawn to process by such fastidious devices as the loose tacking of the horsehair at the top of the skirt as well as the increasing twisting and tacking of it across the body of the skirt and toward the skirt bottom, its final flat anchoring point. Significantly, with such attention to the techniques of the couture, Dior also introduced a nonchalance, stopping the horsehair several inches above the hem. The rippling play of braid that contrasts with its fine mousseline ground is a standard Dior paradox.

In overall impression, the gown assumes the awe-inspiring shape of the grand triangular-skirted dresses of the 1860s. The horsehair tiers further emulate the crinoline circumferences of the mid-nineteenth century.

1952

Evening dress, detail, 1952–53. Pink silk net completely covered with opalescent white sequins and pink horsehair braid. Gift of Mrs. David Kluger, 1960 (CI 60.21.3). See also page 109.

This lustrous, short, strapless evening dress is smothered in swirling forms and sequins. Dior completed the extravagance with a grand yet subtle gesture at the lowest register of the embroidered dress: to finish a matte border, he created a band at the hem veiled by a layer of tulle.

Dior's field of sequins is composed of four different styles. Their complex distribution across the field thus creates subtle shifts of light through texture. The result is tone-on-tone simplicity, without sacrifice of brilliance.

was a year of enormous success for Dior. His clothing was being acclaimed internationally, often for its method of seasonal change in exemplification of the constantly new. Early controversies were more or less forgotten. In the spring, the "Sinuous Line" collection was announced, and in the fall, the "Profile Line." These collections embodied the genial, familiar Dior; they retreated a little toward basic shape and little decoration after the grandiose textile treatments of the previous year. Acclaimed for the new and glamorous, Dior was now delving into his own conventions and developing ever more nuanced treatments of his favorite themes. His sweater dresses, shirtwaists, and versatile cocktail and early-evening ensembles were seized upon as being new, though all previously had been part of Dior's evolving repertoire. Having allowed the waist to rise in 1950 and 1951, Dior frequently used a cummerbund-like wrapping to create a wide waistband that could at once visually accommodate both the natural waist and the raised waist. Ties at the waist were especially common, yoking the idea of both the cummerbund or obilike wrap and the architectonics of the dress. The "La Cigale" dance dress (see page 106), for instance, demonstrates this type of tie at the waist, which serves as a joist between bust-thrust bodice and hipbone-cantilevered skirt.

Skin returned significantly in Dior's work in 1952. After his less exposed earlier collections, evening wear for 1952 was often strapless and very revealing. Throughout his career, Dior flirted with the provocation of showing the body. In both his day dresses and evening dresses, décolletage was often daring, though usually mitigated with a scarf or inset. Some collections were simply more boldly naked than others; in 1952, he loved a controlled exposure of the body. Accompanying bared skin was another manifestation of nature, one of Dior's favorites, flowers. Floral motives, both realistic and abstracted, were important this year. Though they appeared in both printed and elaborately woven textiles, flowers came most ostentatiously to bloom with the collaboration of Dior and the skilled embroiderers at his service.

Day dress and shoulder detail, 1952. Black wool. Gift of Mrs. Benjamin Shaw, 1974 (1974.258.1 a-c)

Dior's penchant for button as ornament flourishes in this day dress. Here, Dior alludes to the plastron fronts of military jackets, with their multiple buttons that were once functional. The Dior bodice buttons at either raglan shoulder line. Its angled stance is mirrored in the button closures at the skirt's upper hipline, furthering the visual allusion to the curved button placement on nineteenth-century uniforms and even to the drop-front pants most associated with sailors.

This detail of the shoulder shows an additional technical complication: what appears to be a jewel neckline is in fact a tiny band inserted to create a trompe-l'oeil collar. Other designers, such as Chanel and Schiaparelli, embraced a theatrical, conspicuous use of trompe l'oeil; Dior saves his covert mirage in the details for God's eye.

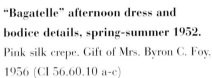

**"Bagatelle" afternoon dress and
bodice details, spring-summer 1952.**
Pink silk crepe. Gift of Mrs. Byron C. Foy,
1956 (CI 56.60.10 a-c)

This afternoon dress with a scooped neckline is a tour de force of tucking and pleating. The bodice is constructed of horizontal
welt tucks, and the skirt is composed of
densely layered pleats that form a complex
box pleat. For all the simplicity of the

effect, one can still see the technical
sophistication in the resolution of such
details as concealed handmade buttonholes
and pattern pieces that violate conventional
seaming—elements especially noticeable
where the neckline band wraps at the cap
sleeve. In the early 1950s, Dior endeav-
ored to reinforce his theme of innocence
and the *jeune fille*, and it is those qualities
that this complicated, though seemingly
plain and simple, dress demonstrates.

"Jean Pierre Grédy" cocktail emsemble and bodice detail, 1952. Black silk taffeta and red silk chiffon. Gift of Lisa and Jody Greene, in memory of their loving mother, Ethel S. Greene, 1958 (CI 58.13.8 a-c)

As with many of Dior's ensembles, it is an option and a challenge on the part of the wearer to determine how she wears this one. Worn with its jacketlike wrap, it appears to be a dress, but removing the wrap surprisingly reveals a skirt and blouse beneath. A tiny line of fuchsia chiffon peaks out amidst the expansive black taffeta; that scarflike edge is a fully realized underbodice that has been wrapped and gathered into a fixed fichu neckline and cummerbund waist. Normally, fitted and tailored effects are created through cutting and piecing rather than draping.

"La Cigale" dance dress and waistline detail, fall-winter 1952. Gray moiré ottoman. Gift of Irene Stone, in memory of her daughter, Mrs. Ethel S. Greene, 1959 (CI 59.26.3 a.b)

Harper's Bazaar (September 1952) described "La Cigale" as built in "gray moiré, so heavy it looks like pliant metal," while *Vogue* (September 1, 1952) called it "a masterpiece of construction and execution." In 1952, what has been called the Dior slouch was placed inside a severe International Style edifice. The devices customarily used to soften surface and silhouette in Dior are eschewed, and the dress becomes the housing of the fashionable posture now required by its apparent weight: the skirt is cantilevered at the hipbone—hip forward, stomach in, shoulders down, and the back long and rounded. Dior employed shaped pattern pieces to mold the bodice to the body and likewise to allow for the dilation at the hips.

Evening dress, 1952–53. Pink silk net completely covered with opalescent white sequins and pink horsehair braid. Gift of Mrs. David Kluger, 1960 (CI 60.21.3)

Dior conceived a garment irrevocably and impeccably brought it to completion with the conceptual certainty of an abstract painter. Edges on a Dior dress are definite, even those with the most extravagant embellishment. Dior's imposition of a net band at the neckline of this dress, along with the net-veiled hem, intimates an aesthetic goal in addition to a refined perimeter between skin and dress. Dior knew the fashion tradition of a transitional zone between garment and skin found in Second Empire borders of net and lace. In fact, his silhouette here is like that of a truncated 1860s dress built out by means of a crinoline support. Also in the manner of nineteenth-century court dress is Dior's composition of shaping in ever more elegant layers. The skirt achieves its volume with three strata: a white net petticoat stiffened with horsehair, another net petticoat with a hemline ruffle, and a slip of white silk crêpe.

"Vilmorin" dress, spring-summer 1952. Ivory silk organza with green, red, and white silk floss and yellow silk chenille. Gift of Mrs. Byron C. Foy, 1955 (CI 55.76.20a-d)

The lush field of French daisies, sown by the embroiderer, serves to accentuate the waist by contrasting the remarkable austerity of the belt against a dense three-dimensional patterning. While the flowers, depicted in bud and in full bloom, are scattered wildly over seam lines, darts, and other details of construction—obliterating and beautifying them—they also fade in number toward the neckline and hemline. The dress is thereby conceived as a pictorial plane with defined margins. That the design graduates into plain cloth at the hem and disappears under a similarly plain bertha collar at the neckline suggests the couturier's priorities: to create a garment of beauty, but one that does not compete with the beauty of the client. For all the decorative exuberance of the embroidery, it is simple white cloth that frames the client's face, neck, and poitrine, and that borders the exposed length of leg.

"Odette" ball gown, fall-winter 1952.
White silk satin with flock-printed black
carnations. Gift of Mrs. Byron C. Foy,
1955 (CI 55.76.24)

Printing a graphic black floral design on
white suggests Edwardian dress, but the
silhouette of this gown has the bell shape
of the 1860s, employing its own interior
structure of corset and skirt-buttressing
crinolines and also requiring padding at
the hips for full realization of the form.
The historical amalgam this dress implies
is furthered by an account in *Vogue*
(February 15, 1954) that Mrs. Foy wore
it to a David-Weill debut party held in
the vacated Fifth Avenue mansion that
had been the last residence of Mrs.
Cornelius Vanderbilt. *Vogue* reported that
the evening had the "look of an Edith
Wharton party," an effect to which this
dress could only have contributed.

1953

"Caracas" dinner dress, detail, spring-summer 1953. Red-and-green floral-printed silk organza. Gift of Mr. and Mrs. Henry Rogers Benjamin, 1954 (CI 65.14.6 a-c). See also page 125.

After the intense armature that characterized 1952, 1953 arrived as gently as a spring rain. Relaxed, negligible fabrics introduced an element of suppleness largely unwanted the year before. In "Caracas," a dress honoring the 1953 opening of a Dior salon in Venezuela, a shirred seam with thin bands of translucent horsehair ribbon gives each flounce a bounce. Dior named garments for places important to him, not for business reasons but for evocative value. The fluid dancing quality of this dress connotes Latin spirit.

signaled Dior's reckoning with natural shapes. The spring collection was the "Tulip," while fall originated the "Cupola." The architecture of Etienne Louis Boullée as well as the folly of gazebos were at the time supremely Dior, who combined a strong eighteenth-century historicism with a *jardinier*'s delight. The year afforded a startling freedom for Dior. The refreshed and innocent garden that had begun in 1952 was cultivated in every way in 1953. Severe in many ways in earlier years, Dior now opened up a natural and painterly garden by means of dresses like "May" (see page 120) with its *jeune fille* innocence and "Caracas" (see page 125) with its lush approximation of landscape painting. The "Tuileries" day coat (see page 117) celebrates a garden even more than history; it takes on the schematic of a formal garden, as opposed to the exotic and wild gardens that are called to mind by other garments in the collection.

Dior's distinctly modern garden is both contemporary and primal at once. It hints at a reference to the Garden of Eden and a state of innocent joy, without repression or vulgarity. It manifests, as well, the ideal of a modern postwar world through its nonchalance and democratic style.

Dior was less an autocrat than an aristocrat. He believed in etiquette and propriety. But he was also a gardener. In 1953, supplanting handfuls of earth with rich fistsfuls of silk, he created a garden pristine and unaffected. The paradox is that the man who

"Tuileries" day coat, fall-winter 1953.
Black-and-red wool. Courtesy Barbara
Barondess MacLean

While other dresses of the year were
named for exotic sites, the "Tuileries"
day coat is as ardently French as the
Marseillaise. The combination of red and
black evokes a Stendhal or Dumas
romance, the former evident in the cross
and colors, the latter manifest in a *Three
Musketeers* shape. The axial disposition
of red suggests the formality of French
garden schemes and underscores the
allusive and narrative possibilities Dior
gained in naming his designs.

Hat, 1953. Black velour with black ostrich and jet-bead trimmed brush aigrettes. Gift of Irma Torem, 1981 (1981.72.1)

Despite the presence of sumptuous feathers and jet beads, this hat was shown with a narrow late-day suit. Dior styled his hats both to complement and as paradox to his outfits. Aigrettes, often referential to early-twentieth-century millinery, are here stubby and dense. They more likely relate to Dior's penchant for feminizing menswear for women to wear. Thus, a Tyrolean badger-brush hat ornament is suggested in this unequivocally ladylike version.

with such successful artifice reconfigured and obscured the female form cultivated gardens always with the allusion to Eden, a sunny paradise where clothing was a superfluous encumbrance.

In the fall collection, belts, bows, and cummerbunds again disguised Dior's rising waistline, while tightly fitted bodices and open necklines also continued to accentuate the bust. In addition, the spring "Mexico" and "Caracas" dinner dresses (see pages 122 and 125) introduced subtle references to regional dress. For example, the short puffed sleeves and the wrapping toward the side of their skirts enhance the playfully peasantlike silhouettes.

Dior's uses of geographical references as dress titles are invariably removed from any geopolitics. Dior strove to be apolitical even as he cited cities and countries of the world. It is hard to imagine a purer, more aestheticized travelogue oblivious to the political world.

"May" evening gown and detail, spring-summer 1953. Ivory silk organza with green-and-purple silk-floss embroidery. Gift of Mrs. David Kluger, 1960 (CI 60.21.1ab)

Dior reveled in the paradox of the natural and the sophisticated. The most telling example of this is in his frequent self-presentation, not as a man who to the world symbolized the authority of French taste, but rather as a simple gardener,

farmer, and mill owner.

In "May," flowering grasses and wild clover are rendered in silk floss on organza. That this "simple" patterning of meadow-gone-to-weed is composed of the tiniest French knots and the meticulously measured stitches of the hand embroiderer suggests that for Dior it was not only that beauty resides in the most rustic but also that the most successful artifice is a beguiling and ostensible naivete.

"Mexico" dinner dress, spring-summer 1953. Black-and-white printed silk organza. Gift of Mr. and Mrs. Henry Rogers Benjamin, 1965 (CI 65.14.7 a-c)

The ample, softly wrapped skirt of the "Mexico" dress as well as its bodice suggest a peasant skirt and blouse. Dior's ever-present capacity to evoke simple clothing, even as he brought it to elegant circumstance in textile and construction, is operative. The print resembles stylized broderie anglaise and is among the simplest of print patterns.

The skirt pattern spirals around, layering the organza upon itself without end. Elsewhere, Dior provided substantial substructure. Here, the support is continuous with the exposed fabric.

"Caracas" dinner dress, spring-summer 1953. Red-and-green floral-printed silk organza. Gift of Mr. and Mrs. Henry Rogers Benjamin, 1954 (CI 65.14.6 a-c)

Dior took advantage of the pliant fabric with a huge spiral that begins at the left hip; the flounces increase in width as they wrap around the body in the skirt.

Sister dress to "Mexico," this dinner dress depends on the languid drape of the organza. Each tier is gathered into the next and supported by horsehair bands. The fluidity and volume of the skirt evoke the movement of dance.

127

"Eventail" cocktail dress and waistline detail, 1953. Midnight- and royal-blue floral-patterned silk taffeta. Gift of Muriel Rand, 1963 (CI 63.36 a-c)

Of course, the fan, as an expressive accessory of court flirtation and communication, was held in the hand, but Dior incorporated it into the dress. The flourish at the

waist acts as ornament, as does the bow on an obi, which, however, is more typically placed at back. Dior, emphasizing the midriff as a focal point, utilized a dramatic detail to focus the eye on the waist.

The fan's role is one to which Dior would have been very sensitive. The aegis and instrument of powerful and coquettish women, it both conceals and discloses.

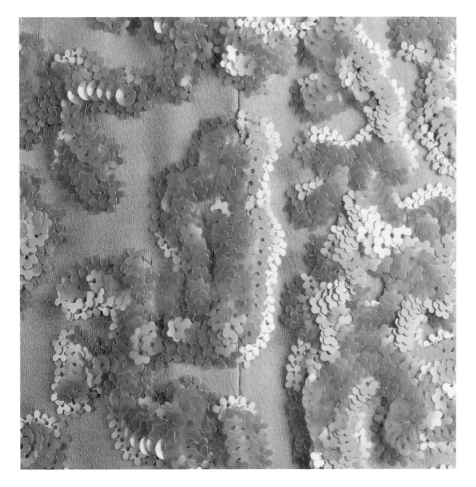

"Annapurna" evening dress and detail, fall-winter 1953. White silk satin with clusters of translucent and white sequins. Gift of Mrs. Byron C. Foy, 1955 (CI 55.76.13)

Tiny flower clusters blanket a heavily sequined surface, whose nacreous quality is the consequence of two different daisy-shaped sequins, one translucent and the other chalk-white. The combination pro-duces an apparent mother-of-pearl effect that enhances the sheen of the satin ground. White on white was as much a part of Dior's thinking as it was of Russian abstract painter Kazimir Malevich's. Rhinestone, sequin, or embroidery orna-ment on a textile surface was used by Dior to articulate an immense variety of white fields, very much like Malevich's compositions of infinite planes in versa-tile white.

Ball gown and bodice detail, fall-winter 1953. Pale-pink silk satin with allover opalescent-pink sequin-and-pearl embroidery. Gift of Mrs. Byron C. Foy, 1955 (CI 55.76.23)

The richly surfaced embroidery mitigates the almost austere simplicity and frontality of this gown. Only in profile does the extravagant fullness of the back of the skirt show its inherent opulence.

Overall embroideries of this kind depend upon a general template, but the irregular pattern is in the realm of the embroiderer. Nineteen-fifties painting has a like sense of deliberate randomness within the overall.

Ball gown and detail, spring-summer 1953. Pink silk satin and embroidered tulle. Gift of Mrs. Byron C. Foy, 1955 (CI 55.76.22 a-c)

Not since the House of Worth in the Belle Époque has a designer carried a love of the barely perceived detail to such extravagant extreme. A veil of tulle dulls the shimmer of the satin ground but then is embellished with a scalloped web of silver seed beads and pendant crystals. Excess and obsession govern the selection of ornamental elements.

The waist is emphasized as the point of convergence of the scallops: in the bodice, the swags drop down; on the skirt, the scallops work upward.

"Lelia" ball gown (worn as a wedding gown), front view, detail, and back view, spring-summer 1953. Pale-gray silk satin with silver braid and rhinestone embroidery. Gift of Jean Sinclair Tailer. 1964 (CI 64.13.1)

This dress is one of a number of designs photographed to appear in *Life* Magazine as appropriate dress for the Coronation of Queen Elizabeth II of England. The Belle Époque decorum and sweep of the back of the skirt signify courtliness. The apparent dip of the center-back alters the proportion of the torso and obscures the natural waist, thus creating the attenuated silhouette of the late nineteenth century. A Diorism occurs in the structure of the neckline as it wraps over the shoulder: it is, in fact, not anchored to the bodice itself, as Dior vacillated between the rigid and the loose in his garments. Mobility is made possible by a slit at center-front beginning at the knee. The two pleated back panels, suggesting the draped backs of 1890s ball gowns, are continuations of the pattern pieces of the Princesse-style front. A fully constructed back skirt functions as an anchor to this vestige of a train.

1954

"Compiègne" ball gown, detail, fall-winter 1954. Slate-blue silk satin velour au sabre. Gift of Mrs. Byron C. Foy, 1956 (CI 56.60.7). See also page 156

By tacking the soft fabric to a rigid underbodice in frozen folds, the designer took full advantage of the attributes of the dress, combining strict silhouette and lissome flow. The fabric spirals around the body in a torque of drapery that is only possible through the surety of an infrastructure.

is the year when Dior's collections were difficult to characterize. His spring collection, "Lily of the Valley," included dresses with his favored flower, but there were also dresses and suits with masculine tailoring and materials. The eponymous dress of the collection suggests the lily of the valley in its crisp white silk faille but has nothing of the springtime profligacy of the garden dresses of prior collections. If anything, this is the flower rendered conceptual, not florist-fresh. Dior's fall collection, the "H-line," justified by its creator as being inspired by the figure of a young girl, was, in fact, less like the *jeune fille* than his sweet dresses of the year before. One wonders if there was not even a desired befuddlement in these collections of misnomer descriptions. Likewise, the "Priscilla" evening dress (see page 145) may indicate that, in the fall collection, the silhouette was more about shape than about sweet youth.

Menswear invaded the garden with a powerful force in spring 1954. A sailor collar went out for evening, while chalk-stripes on navy-blue and gray and "smoking" (tuxedo) blacks-on-black usurped the man's business and evening suits to become women's tailoring and cocktail dresses. Straw boaters and sailor caps were prevalent in the millinery. After sporadic intrusions of such menswear paradigms into Dior's work, menswear became an unfailing presence in 1954. Ironically, Gabrielle Chanel is often given credit for establishing borrowings from menswear as one of her early influences. Chanel had just returned to design at this

"Benjamin" day dress and detail, spring-summer 1954. Navy-blue wool crêpe. Gift of Mr. and Mrs. Henry Rogers Benjamin, 1965 (CI 65.14.10 a-d)

In what otherwise might be a conventional suit, the Diorism is at the neckline. A polymorphic ambiguity occurs at that location, creating uncertainty between inner and outer garment. The suit jacket features a high square neckline cut to accommodate a scarf or to be worn with a separate trompe-l'oeil sailor collar that raises the neck closure and results in a tailored flourish that encodes a more decorous ensemble.

Cartwheel hat, 1954. Black fur felt and velvet. Gift of Varney Thompson Elliott and Rosemary Thompson Franciscus, in memory of their mother, Margaret Whitney Thompson, 1985 (1985.365.33)

As is true of Dior's tailoring and dressmaking, his hats also benefit from close inspection as well as from the view from afar. A bow that might seem extrinsic to the design is really inherent to the construction of the crown. Black fur felt is molded into the scallop form of the cartwheel. Light and shadow, endemic to the appearance of any hat, are intensified in the contrast between the nap of the felt brim against the darker, light-absorbing pile of the velvet. Thus, within the great halo of the cartwheel, Dior played black on black, shadow on bottomless shadow, making us aware of the luxury of the constituent materials.

time; she and Dior saw themselves as antipodes in fashion. Yet the woman designer inspired by men's tailoring and the male designer responsible for archetypal femininity in the 1950s were not so far apart. Their dissimilar paths converged in their mutual pillaging of menswear.

Yet, as always, it is incorrect to seek to connect Dior's work with that of his contemporaries. Dior was a designer of intense self-involvement, never influenced by those outside of his own atelier. Whatever else happened in the fashion world in Dior's time was either indebted to him or independent of him, but Dior was invariably oblivious to others in the fashion world. Thus, the serendipity of menswear influences is not a conscious competition in any way.

By 1954, Dior was recognized as one of the great artistic masters of France and a prime force in the postwar renaissance. Dior's chateau-named dresses are a particular fantasy that allowed him to combine his penchant for the bucolic aura of regional France with the grand style of historical France. In such grand terms, Dior also set out the chateaux as a landscape of national pride and patrimony. His cartwheel hats suggested the majestic scale; his recourse to ever-more extravagant refinement was like that of the campaigns of building the chateaux, each to surpass the other in modernity and in palatial effect.

"Muguet" evening dress, spring-summer 1954. White silk faille. Gift of Mrs. Byron C. Foy, 1955 (CI 55.76.15 a-c)

While Dior's respected but rival couturier, Cristobal Balenciaga, is identified more with the balloon or harem-hemmed dress, this association is in part due to Balenciaga's hyperbolic interpretation of that construction. In fact, Dior's love of the natural fall and hang of fabric made unpressed folding a natural gesture, and the balloon dress was its inevitable outcome.

"Priscilla" evening dress and details, fall-winter 1954. Light brown-and-beige silk satin. Gift of Mrs. Benjamin Shaw. 1974 (1974.258.7)

The volume of every Dior dress is sustained by underpinnings, some permanently attached and others detachable. In "Priscilla," a separate crinoline is not required, as layers of chiffon-lined net support the drop-waist fullness of the dress. Even in such structural elements, the beautiful finishing techniques of the couture atelier are visible. Indicative of the "H-line" silhouette in which corsetry created a radically different profile for the bust, seeming to flatten the chest and unusually widening the upper torso, "Priscilla" underscores the horizontal effect with a straight neckline.

**"Luxembourg" coat, front and back
views, spring-summer 1954.** White silk
faille with black silk-velvet trim. Gift of
Mrs. Byron C. Foy, 1956 (CI 56.60.9)

Like other art of its time, Dior's did not
seize a definite and indisputable reading
but waxed greater with multivalent possibilities. His clothing forms are suggestive,
often expressing a range including both

contemporary culture and historical
dress. A contemporaneous sailor collar is
imposed on this evening coat. The deep-
cuffed bell-shaped sleeve, kimonolike
wrap, and back fullness of this same coat
offer a faint reference to late-seventeenth-
century mantuas. Dior preferred neither
sailor nor mantua as exclusive analogue:
he inferred a broader sense of allusion.

"Arsène Lupin" theater dress, fall-winter 1954. Black wool broadcloth and silk satin. Gift of Christian Dior, 1955 (CI 55.29.2 a,b)

If theater traditionally had been a place for licensed cross-dressing, Dior took that opportunity to create a woman's alternative to a man's "smoking." Instead of satin lapels, he utilized a black satin ribbon. Of course, Dior's treatment is the most discreet possible, as were his earlier transformations of gray flannel suits to womenswear. This dress originally was shown with a long satin coat of seven-eighths length.

"Nuit de Rêve" evening dress, underdress detail, and underdress, spring-summer 1954. Pale-lavender silk organza. Gift of Mr. and Mrs. Henry Rogers Benjamin, 1965 (CI 65.14.9)

From 1947 on, Dior practiced a stratified construction, building out from a firm inner structure. By 1954, he was thinking more in terms of fluid, tissuelike layers. This evening dress has a sheer skin over a completely finished underdress in the identical fabric. In addition, the underdress is fortified by a layer of net.

In contrast to his earlier evening dresses, Dior here continued the "Princesse" seaming that allows for an unbroken line at the waist. The only presence of a break at the torso and hips is the loosely gathered bow knot.

**"Nuit d'Août" ball gown, spring-sum-
mer 1954.** White silk chiffon printed
with yellow-rose and green-leaf clusters.
Gift of Mrs. Byron C. Foy, 1956
(CI 56.60.5 a-d)

Dior's evocation of the ancien régime is
clear in this silhouette. He played on the
idea of a polonaise of that era by using
an overdress that pulls up to reveal an
underskirt. In this case, what actually
makes the draping at both sides is an
unbroken length of chiffon tacked into
the waist at back and falling away into
two separate trains, but the impression is
that of the grand court shape. The overall
pattern abets the evocation of a rococo
design.

"Nuit Fraiche" ball gown and detail, spring-summer 1954. Pale-blue silk faille embroidered with polychrome silk floss and sequins. Gift of Mrs. Byron C. Foy, 1956 (CI 56.60.4 a-d)

Dior frequently used the strapless gown as the basis from which to create alterable effects modifiable by the use of jackets and stoles. Here, a half-jacket (literally two armholes and a capelet) transforms the neckline of the gown. The detail above shows a typical couture resolution: embroidery is used to obliterate the separate pattern pieces through a camouflaging of the seaming.

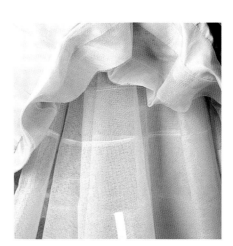

"Compiègne" ball gown and detail, fall-winter 1954. Slate-blue satin velour au sabre. Gift of Mrs. Byron C. Foy, 1956 (CI 56.60.7)

Summer residence of France's kings and queens and royal hunting grounds for centuries, Compiègne is a richly evocative place. In one of Dior's last great historicist collections, he used the mystique of Compiègne for a dress with the silhouette of the crinoline forms of the Second Empire. Its lush textile may also be an homage to the long history of such French silks and dress fabrics. Although the undeniable focus of this gown is the virtuoso wet-draping effect of the bodice, the subtle center-front inverted skirt pleat recalls Dior's earlier interest in scissorlike construction.

"Chambord" ball gown and detail, fall-winter 1954. Gray silk tulle with pearl, rhinestone, and sequin embroidery. Gift of Mrs. Byron C. Foy, 1957 (CI 57.29.5)

Another dress in the chateau series, the "Chambord" ball gown, is girdled with an elaborate mix of sequins and beads.

A Diorism evident in this gown is the heavy encrustation that fades gradually to yards and layers of ethereal tulle. The lavish concentration of paillettes is a convergence of two of Dior's great signatures: decorative emphasis of the waist and the desire to ombré surface ornament away from the midriff.

1955

"Soirée de New York" evening dress, detail, fall-winter 1955. Burgundy silk velvet with gunmetal bead embroidery. Gift of Mrs. Byron C. Foy, 1957 (CI 57.29.1). See also page 175.

Dior delighted in the capabilities of the couture hand. Generally preferring random distribution of adornment and the gradual diminution of decorative elements toward margins, he made an exception in this case to offer what seems a highly regular and routine pattern. But he knew the effect of these angled lines: embroidery in crisscrossing seed beads provides that light will always hit one angled line of beading, guaranteeing that there is always a shimmer in every zone. Dior designed for the candlelight of ancien régime evenings even in the electric century.

saw the acme of Dior's upheaval. He announced the "A-line" for spring. That silhouette, suspended from a narrow shoulder, triangulated out from a crossbar at the waist and continued to splay out to the hem. The "Princesse" line had portended this moment of Dior amendment, but no collection had so wholly challenged the New Look's fundamentals. In the fall, the "Y-line" ensued, shifting mass, and thus focus, back to the upper body.

To review the Dior "A-line" of 1955 is to see the future foreshadowed in this season's most demure genesis. A tunic jacket lugged down the line of a waist in the "A-line" suit; it was hardly the full version of the reductive "A-line" dresses of late 1950s and the 1960s. The ultimate flaring out was initially very reserved.

The turnaround in silhouette that occurred from spring to fall in 1955 is a token of the capriciousness that is often charged against fashion. Dior scarcely deserved such a rebuke, for his collections were more continuous and evolving in their design than they were in their rhetorical shifts. But in 1955, the "Y-line" was a contrivance. Dior had always focused his attention on the upper body and the zone of the waist. Designer Geoffrey Beene has rightly observed that Dior often seemed to lose interest in a dress after he worked his way down to the waistline. But more massive collars and shoulders seemed an erratic return in 1955, just after the sandwich reduction to the "A-line" silhouette. The "Virevolte" ensemble (see pages 168 and 169) and the "Mayfair" ensemble

"Sinbad" casque, 1955. Raspberry-pink fur felt. Gift of Mrs. Byron C. Foy. 1956 (CI 56.60.11)

This snug helmetlike casque is more a point of punctuation than a complete sentence. Yet Dior parses even the smallest element of style into it. by technical means (radiating seams) and also by using bold color as accentuation much as he did in other accessories. If the shape is a flattened Diorized fez. the pink is a Diorization of the fez's traditional crimson.

(see pages 170 and 171), for example, suggest Dior's talent for adding interest and magnitude at the upper chest and shoulder without suffocating his women.

By the mid-1950s, Dior was often taken to be an oracle on the discipline and future of fashion. The sweetness and devotion to atelier techniques that inhabit the dresses, as much in these years as initially, are also innate in his writings. Amidst changing design schema, he maintained an unerring sense of fashion as a sacred legacy, writing that "the maintenance of the tradition of fashion is in the nature of an act of faith. In a century which attempts to tear the heart out of every mystery, fashion guards its secret well, and is the best possible proof there is still magic abroad." Between the discourse and the work, there is some variation, as Dior's enchanted proclamations of this period made little notice of the change he was affecting in his work to come to terms with a new form. He never disavowed the public's expectations of magic in both the process and ambition of fashion, but Dior was far less complacent than he feigned.

"A" ensemble, spring-summer 1955.
Gray silk-and-wool flannel. Gift of
Christian Dior, 1955 (CI 55.63 a-c)

A model primarily remembered for having been in the wedding trousseau of
Olivia de Haviland, this gray wool suit is
the transfiguration of the man's suit as an
expression of the feminine. More importantly, this suit, long anticipated by Dior's
interest in tailoring and in menswear fabrics, is poised on the edge of Dior's move
away from the New Look's historicism
toward a simpler, increasingly reductive,
architectonic geometry. The essential A-
line of the 1960s began here.

Day dress and detail, spring-summer 1955. Periwinkle-blue silk. Gift of Mrs. David Kluger, 1960 (CI 60.21.4 a-c)

This dress typifies Dior's incorporation of opposites—covered and bared, fitted and flared. In particular, Dior commanded a huge repertoire of pleats. By folding he was able to emphasize the fabric's natural weight and "hand." His ability to compress a volume was coupled with his invention of decorative effect from the process—here, sunburst pleats. Dior's principle is modern: decoration is the requirement and responsibility of structure, not an appendage. Yet the work appears at first to be more complicated than the corresponding vocabulary of architecture and design.

**"Virevolte" ensemble, with and
without jacket, fall-winter 1955.**
Black-and-white wool twill. Gift of
Mrs. Hans H. Zinsser. 1965
(CI 65.21.3 a-d)

The fall-winter 1955 collection displayed
an attribute long imagined by Dior: dress
as a musical composition, variably harmo-

nious with and without jackets and wraps.
Further. Dior's study in layering involves
a trompe-l'oeil neckline. Rather than his
more usual device of an outer garment
incorporating a faux scarf. this dress has
an open-necked jacket that allows for a
jabotlike view of the underbodice. The
jabot is not applied but rather is config-
ured by the insertion of darts and tucks.

"Mayfair" ensemble, with and without jacket, fall-winter 1955. Black wool with mink trim. Gift of Mrs. Byron C. Foy. 1957 (CI 57.29.7 a-d)

One ensemble can generate two very different effects. An outer jacket with a finished fur outline and trimmed with a bow creates a suit appropriate for late day or dinner. Underneath, an autonomous cocktail dress can easily be worn with another garment or with the jacket. The will to such versatility in dressing was for Dior manifestly not about sparing clients either money or the need for more wardrobe items; it was about an aesthetic economy, a desire to see the harmony of parts.

To create additional interest to the waist, Dior cropped the jacket to reveal a glimmer of the contoured satin belt.

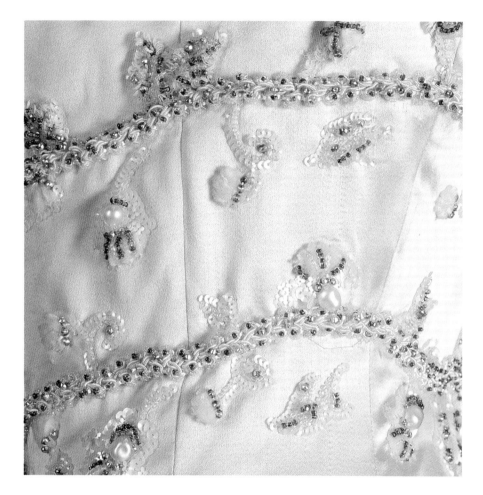

"Petite Soirée" evening dress and detail, fall-winter 1955. Pale-pink silk satin with white braid, bead, and sequin embroidery. Gift of Mrs. Byron C. Foy, 1957 (CI 57.29.4)

Horizontal lines of embroidery exaggerate the cantilevered thrust of the skirt, demonstrating Dior's new architectural and reductive mode. Construction lines are obscured, though, by the overlay of embroidery. As in many Dior gowns, the back view reveals a dramatic flourish of fabric that is unexpected given the simplicity and austerity of the shaped front. Without sacrificing his long-standing interest in historical gowns, Dior has created one that is more Saarinen than Second Empire.

"Soirée de New York" evening dress, fall-winter 1955. Burgundy silk velvet with gunmetal bead embroidery. Gift of Mrs. Byron C. Foy, 1957 (CI 57.29.1)

Dior's decisively unobstructed geometry of 1955 achieves essential definition through shape, assuming a dramatic boldness of silhouette. Unlike many earlier instances of the complex variegation of ornament on the surface, Dior's resolution during that year was to take an overall embroidery and to treat the whole of the dress like a unified canvas. The embroidery is so thoroughly mitred over the seam lines that the dress seems to be an indivisible integer. The new torso shaping, "Princesse" construction, and cupola skirt are combined.

Evening dress, fall-winter 1955. Black silk satin with silk velvet sash. Gift of Mr. and Mrs. Henry Rogers Benjamin, 1965 (CI 65.14.12 a,b)

Exemplifying Dior's faultless minimalism of 1955, this simple black column, contrasting matte velvet against satin, anticipates a form of evening dress that has continued to the present. The stability of the off-the-shoulder neckline is accomplished by the customized shaping of the pattern pieces rather than by any rigid understructure. The Dior dress took on a` new suppleness without sacrificing its abiding architectonics.

1956

"Salzbourg" ball gown, detail, fall-winter 1956. Pale-pink silk faille. Purchase, Irene Lewisohn Fund, 1995 (1995.468.4). See also page 189.

In keeping with his long tradition of superimposing a luxurious skin onto a firmly boned corselet, Dior in 1956 used center-front knotting. It is as if the most exterior layer is supple enough to be drawn and knotted over the base of the garment's structure. The folds radiating from the knot supplant the darts and seams required in tailoring to create the shaping of the bust and hips.

is the year when the existing vocabulary of shapes was reified. But also present was the dramatic elevation of the waist. In an unremittingly pretty spring collection, Dior let the high-waisted "Arrow" stand for his directional interest, an innovation accomplished without diminishing the charm of the dresses. The fall collection was given the sentimental title "Aimant," but it continued Dior's campaign to clarify shape. Thus, the romantic evocation bestowed on a dress like the "Salzbourg" ball gown (see page 189) is not entirely true to its emphasis on spare structure. High-waisted and equally elevated in the abstraction of its form, "Salzbourg" expresses utmost modernist simplicity and authenticity. What the 1956 emphasis on structure may have implied was the finality with which Dior was moving away from "The New Look." The higher waist and its resultant proportions constituted a major change for Dior. It was a change that precipitated the *demi-longueur* that arrived in the fall: a long length in skirts and coats, sometimes made awkward by the mass of material falling almost to the ankle.

By 1956, Dior was a fortress. Though he could be assailed by nay-sayers, he had become an established and irrefutable institution. Though he reigned as fashion's dictator, he was discomforted by such authority. This paradox is most apparent in his ability to design collections with both strong focus and great breadth. Nineteen fifty-six was not a year of sameness or

"Ritz" suit, fall-winter 1956. Black wool twill with brown mink trim. Gift of Irene Stone, 1962 (CI 62.52.2 a-c)

Characteristically, Dior composed this suit by combining a complete underdress with a jacket, a coupling that allows for versatile dressing. Yet the style also suggests the easing up of the New Look silhouette: the volume of the skirt is no longer supported by layers of crinoline, though there is still an emphasis on a defined waist.

The "Ritz" suit was originally shown with a prominent self-bow at the center of the waist. While Balenciaga was famous for the thrust back interest of his kimono-like necklines, Dior much preferred the décolleté and portrait necklines that emphasize the bust and the slope of the shoulder.

Hat, 1956. Palm fronds. Gift of Mrs. Alan L. Corey Jr., Mrs. William T. Newbold, and Mrs. A. G. Paine II, 1980 (1980.126.35)

In the modernist spirit of Dior's collections of the mid-1950s, hats often became miniatures of International Style conceptualization. Basic forms prevailed, and the designer's contribution was less in the area of invention than it was in the faculty of construction. Palm fronds are meticulously woven to form a curving dome: a basketweaving process builds a familiar shape out of a surprisingly exotic medium that has been tamed by Dior.

contentment with the past; it was a watershed year for promoting new directions.

As always with Dior, the design probity of his work never suffered from his acclaim. For all those who never wanted him to depart from the natural latitude of the waist, 1956 was either ignored or considered only with regard to its most conservative forms. A collection of some two hundred pieces always provided a selection appropriate for the conservative clients as well as more avant-garde pieces for the more adventuresome. In 1956, Dior's most perspicacious clients were seeing an architectural vision and an anticipation of the proportions of the decade to come. The designer's prescience was remarkably like that of an artist who sets out an aesthetic agenda so enormous and suggestive that it can only be resolved by future generations.

"Noisette" day dress, spring-summer 1956. Navy wool. Gift of David and Susan Biberman from the collection of Hilda S. Biberman. 1982 (1982.401.5 a-c)

More clearly than any other dress in this collection, this one is representative of Dior's introduction of a waistline that would creep up farther and farther. The changed proportions here anticipate the next decade's silhouette of shrunken top and raised waistline. Many have noted the fateful irony of Dior's final collections that look so profoundly to the future in denial of "The New Look" and its lasting presence in his work.

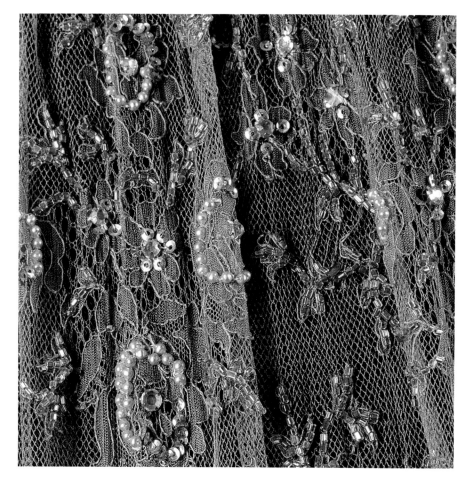

Evening dress and detail, ca. 1956.
Charcoal-gray Chantilly lace heavily
embroidered with silver sequins, rhine-
stones, and glass beads. Gift of
Mrs. David Kluger, 1960 (CI 60.21.2)

Although the chemise shape is chiefly
attributed to Balenciaga, Dior, in fact,
also created dresses in direct opposition
to his usual highly structured silhouettes.

Nonetheless, a vestige of "The New Look"
is still present in the vast amount of
fabric gathered into the waist. Only the
weight of the embroidery on the fragile
ground collapses the skirt into its chemiselike silhouette.

As with "Chérie" (1947; see page 15),
the large volume of fabric at the waist is
turned under on itself to create a flat join
and a softly padded hip support.

**"Salzbourg" ball gown, fall-winter
1956.** Pale-pink silk faille. Purchase,
Irene Lewisohn Fund, 1995
(1995.468.4)

Dior designed a classic A-line gown. The
strapless neckline is made possible by the
stiff bodice, but Dior poised it slightly
away from the body, invoking a lightness
and allowing the dress a floating delicacy
antithetical to its considerable inner
structure. The tie-front, which seems
detached from any understructure, pro-
motes the illusion that the dress is free of
any foundation. The scissorlike construction of earlier collections is merging into
the "A-line."

1957

"Lys Noir" evening gown, detail, fall-winter 1957. Cherry-red silk satin velour au sabre. Gift of Madame Walther Moreira Salles, 1969 (CI 69.39). See also pages 202 and 203.

Because of his desire to create the effect of the grandest amounts of material pinched into a compact form, Dior used a piped seam to define a panel that is gathered and suggests a continuation of the fabric that comprises the body of the gown. The original dress in black reeked of fin-de-siècle aestheticism, but by substituting the same lily-strewn fabric in cherry red, it now suggests Golden Age opulence.

is the final year, but it was marked by promise more than by finality. In rapid revolutions, Dior executed the "Libre" and "Fuseau" collections, projected to liberate the garment from any vestigial jurisdiction of "The New Look" and move back to emphasis on the essence of cloth itself. After a decade, Dior was making a wholly new beginning. It was not his fate to be able to pursue these new and fertile directions, but fashion of the late 1950s and 1960s would be cued by these last collections created by the designer who had unequivocally commanded the 1950s.

By 1957, Dior was showing mammoth collections. It would be difficult to describe coherence among the many options of such a collection, but "Libre" plainly showed a systematic exploration of a softer waist. Dior also invoked the East as much as his beloved European tradition in examples of narrow tunics and sarilike wraps with continuous yards of material and with uninflected waists. Overblouses and long, capacious jackets afforded a chemiselike looseness unlike his earlier fitted silhouettes.

Dior's chemise freedom was always marked by references to white shirting and blouses. The spring collection boasted an unusually large number of fichus, white collars, and sashes that contributed to that sense of freedom, though all of these elements were familiar from Dior's earlier collections. Most importantly, Dior had arrived at a point of convergence with rival couturier Cristobal Balenciaga. Dior respected Balenciaga; he had never regarded this rival with the disparagement he felt for Chanel. In 1957, both designers were feeling the need for a more limber silhouette and lifestyle, and both promoted chemise shapes. In fact, Balenciaga's chemise was more pronounced than that of Dior, but the similarity of the two corresponding silhouettes made for a unified outlook for fashion in 1957.

In fact, Dior suits for fall 1957, such as the "Claro" day ensemble (see pages 194 and 195), possess a blockiness—in avoidance of an easily determined waist—that could be confused with Balenciaga's suits in the period. Dior was not sharing his role as fashion sovereign, and his signature elements of Diorisms remained scattered throughout the collection. His personal reign as fashion's undisputed king ended with a magna carta that made subsequent fashion Dior-based and Dior-inspired for decades to follow.

"Tourbillon" afternoon dress, fall-winter 1957. Black wool crepe. Gift of Mrs. Hans H. Zinsser, 1964 (CI 64.77.1)

An applied bow is a rare element of pure adornment for Dior, but the compelling design element here is the line of cartridge pleats gathered into the dropped waistline. Like "Chérie" (see page 15) from a decade earlier, also an homage to the atelier, the virtuosity of the couture seamstress is apparent in the merging of extraordinary fullness into a flattened and taut expanse of textile.

**"Claro" day ensemble, coat and day
dress without coat, fall-winter 1957.**
Black wool bouclé. Gift of Mr. and Mrs.
Henry Rogers Benjamin, 1965
(CI 65.14.18 a-c)

With this ensemble, Dior posed a layered
repudiation of his own New Look

silhouette. The coat, of an exaggerated blockiness, was to be worn over a tubular dress that ignored the waist and barely acknowledged the bust and hipline. A decade after his innovation, Dior was resolutely denouncing the elements that for so long had constituted the identifiers, and even the intrinsics, of his work.

**Day dress with jacket, back-neckline
jacket detail, and day dress without
jacket, fall-winter 1957.** Moss-green
wool twill. Gift of Mrs. Hans H. Zinsser,
1965 (CI 65.21.2 a)

Both jacket and dress possess a trompe-
l'oeil aspect pertaining to draping and
construction techniques. In the coat, a
cowl at the back neckline seems to be a
functional hood. In the bodice of the
chemise dress, a false overblouse is
implied. In a collection that largely
renounced elements of his prior work and
following a decade of refinement of form,
Dior seems to have seized upon a joy for
criticality and questioning. The wool coat
could also seem like the hooded overcoats
and anoraks that would enter urbane
fashion thinking a decade later.

"Venezuela" evening dress and back-waistline detail, fall-winter 1957.
Charcoal-gray silk faille. Gift of Mrs. Michael Blankfort, in memory of her mother, Mrs. William Constable Breed, 1976 (1976.29.28)

What began as sculptural ornament in "Compiègne" (1954; see page 156) resolves itself structurally in this dress. Spiraling gathers reflect the tensions of the surplice draping of the bodice. Dior's adroitness in combining draping and tailoring techniques is evident in the cummerbundlike back closure, in which drapery seems to be resolved in a convention of tailoring. Dior's bold swathes of cloth across the waist function as painterly gestures, marking an X at the waist.

"Tourterelle" evening gown and detail, spring-summer 1957. Changeant pink and green silk taffeta. Gift of Mrs. Pierre David-Weill, 1975 (1975.176.2 a,b)

As evidenced in the construction of the corselet, this dress, whose label reads "Dior spring 1957," is a replacement version of a 1948 original. Like that original, it has a very loose surface fabric basted onto a structured and net-stiffened underskirt. The shoulder straps are gratuitous, as the boned underbodice would be sufficient support for this gown. The original from 1948 was worn by Beatrice David-Weill and is represented in her 1952 portrait by Salvador Dali.

**"Lys Noir" evening gown, front and
back views, fall-winter 1957.** Cherry-
red silk-satin velour au sabre. Gift of
Madame Walther Moreira Salles, 1969
(CI 69.39)

Conceived as a sarong, this is a more formal version of a dress style that had been
offered in earlier collections. Fabric is

wrapped from a back seam with an asymmetrical hem. Dior resolved the asymmetry of the hem, but, in doing so, he lost the width of fabric required to continue into the side drape. As a result, an extra panel is gathered into the side seam to form a free-flowing train. The appearance is of continuous fabric, but, in fact, Dior had to concoct the process.

Afterword

The American sportswriter and novelist Paul Gallico wrote about a Dior dress in *Mrs. 'Arris Goes to Paris* (1957). He described an English charwoman who was so transfixed by a Dior dress that she made it her personal grail to possess such a creation, not to wear but just for its embodiment of the beautiful and luxurious. Dior dresses have held such enchanted power for nearly fifty years.

Dior was dressmaker to optimism, innocence, luxury, and timeless youth. He cut to the purpose of simulating Second Empire and other historical styles, but he was also making menswear, trompe-l'oeil detailing, and soft-to-hard adherences part of the most modern wardrobe.

Fifty years after that accomplishment, some take the contemporary and flinty critical position that Dior imprisoned women in the fetters of hard form and overt, even clichéed, femininity. But Dior offered as well profound freedoms pertinent to the immediate postwar world that he inhabited and dressed. His renaissance in fabric and decorative opulence was an important sign of renewed style for the second half of the twentieth century. His endorsement of and manifestation of luxury meant not that fashion would be arrogant or haughty but only that fashion had survived its greatest disruption since the founding of the House of Worth in the 1850s. For war-weary and war-deprived France, Dior was the single most effective symbol of artistic and commercial survival, offering Paris as a sustained bastion for fashion and luxury.

Dior is more, however, than the electrifying, exhilarating flash of 1947. In subsequent collections, his ideas evolved in a steady process at odds with the expressions of new titles for every season. By the end of his life, he had come full circle to offer a look entirely free of his New Look yet carrying some of its signature gestures.

Long before Dior's brief eleven years as designer for his own house, he had been a dealer in art. It is as if the career we associate with the modern artist influenced Dior's life as a designer. He believed in his medium of fashion and took its materials to their utmost expression. He believed in his subject, feminine grace, and rendered it powerful and unforgettable. He believed in his métier and employed every device of accomplishment for his art, making it lavish and/or true. And he believed in his epoch, creating around a troubled century's midpoint, garments and an ethos of beauty that remain vivid today.

Bibliography

Ballard, Bettina. *In My Fashion.* New York: David McKay, 1960.

de Marly, Diana. *Christian Dior.* New York: Holmes & Meier, 1990.

"Dictator by Demand." *Time,* March 4, 1957.

Dior, Christian. *Talking about Fashion.* London: Hutchinson, 1954.

———. *Christian Dior and I.* New York: E. P. Dutton, 1957.

Giroud, Françoise. *Dior.* New York: Rizzoli, 1987.

Keenan, Brigid. *Dior in Vogue.* New York: Harmony Books, 1981.

Musée des Arts de la Mode. *Hommage à Christian Dior, 1947-1957.* Paris, 1987.

Perreau, Genevieve. *Christian Dior.* Paris: Helpé, 1953.

Pochna, Marie-France. *Christian Dior: The Man Who Made the World Look New.* New York: Arcade Publishers, 1996.

———. *Dior.* New York: Universe Publishing, 1996.

Snow, Carmel, with Mary Louise Aswell. *The World of Carmel Snow.* New York: McGraw-Hill, 1963.